# SHIFTS
## Architecture c
## the 20th centι

Hans Ibelings and Powerho

The Architecture Observer

# CONTENTS

4 **Foreword**

6 **Diminishing returns**

66 **Catalogue**
68 Sinking and rising
72 Bubbles
76 Property prices
80 Out of balance
84 Riding the wave
88 Designed by architects
92 Demographic growth

# FOREWORD

In this publication two narrative lines – from two architects and an architecture critic – converge. Architects are normally projective, critics reflective. In *Shifts* both the critic and the architects engage in reflection and analysis and both the architects and the critic venture into the realm of speculation about what architecture could be. This is based on a shared interest in the question of what is happening in the world. There are plenty of indications that major changes are taking place in Western society, changes that are more comprehensive than the already far-reaching economic chain reaction that began with the sub-prime mortgage collapse in the US. This economic crisis has opened people's eyes to what can be viewed as a bigger story, a story of shifts in numerous spheres, not just economic, but also geopolitical, ecological, demographic and cultural.
These shifts are viewed here from a Western perspective that is predominantly European, even West-European. When global issues are discussed, it is from this restricted point of view, in full awareness of the limitations that every form of Eurocentrism entails, and with the knowledge that what is a problem for Europe is not necessarily, or not to the same extent, and certainly not as critical, an issue in the Americas, Asia, Africa or Australia. What the Western media have designated a global economic crisis, has not had the same impact in every corner of the world, any more than the dramatic economic crises that Russia, Argentina and Indonesia have experienced since the 1990s have been much felt in, say, Western Europe. That Argentina and Indonesia have either partially

or fully overcome their most recent major economic crises, should give hope to all the pessimists who cannot yet see any light at the end of the European tunnel. Speaking of which, that European tunnel does not consist of a single tube. Europe is not a single entity, especially not when it comes to the impact of the recent economic crisis. Ireland is not Norway, the Netherlands not Greece, Poland not Spain. Tolstoy wrote that 'every unhappy family is unhappy in its own way' and the same is true of every country contending with grave or less grave consequences of the current economic crisis.

From an economic perspective, most countries in the old continent are in the same boat as the US; demographically speaking Europe can be compared with Japan; while in cultural terms the entire Western world, including countries like Australia and Canada that escaped the worst of the economic crisis, finds itself faced with the question, what now? Three years ago, the Powerhouse Company's 'Rien ne va plus' exhibition raised the issue of the consequences of the crisis for architecture, with the idea of following this up with an exhibition showing what might emerge in the wake of the excesses of the pre-crisis period. Not only is it still far too early for that follow-up exhibition, which was to have been called 'Faites vos jeux', but it has become increasingly clear that the bursting of the bubble in which architecture found itself, was not the only change taking place. Thus, first an exhibition and publication about 'shifts', of which the current major recession is only one, albeit important, aspect. Architecture is in many ways dependent on and determined by external factors, whether they be economic, demographic, social or cultural. All those spheres are currently experiencing changes that inevitably have and will have significant consequences for architects, architecture and architectural culture.

Charles Bessard, Hans Ibelings, Nanne de Ru, May 2012

# DIMINISHING RETURNS

Frankfurt, Germany.

The 2009 G8 summit, L'Aquila, Italy.

# 1

Ghost suburbs, abandoned building sites, empty office buildings, shopping streets with boarded up shopfronts, To Rent and For Sale signs everywhere. You don't have to look far to see the effects of the economic recession in the urban landscape. The financial crisis that erupted in the United States of America in 2008 and then went on to wreak havoc in Europe, has left unmistakably deep scars in the built environment. But the visible signs of the crisis are not purely the result of the recklessness of bankers or the lack of fiscal discipline in some European countries. There is more going on.

The fact that architects are suddenly getting less work than before the crisis, that there is less construction activity and more empty buildings, is not solely attributable to what began as a mortgage crisis; many of the causes lie deeper, and go back further than four or five years. In a way, the recession has simply accelerated, and exacerbated, various pre-existing trends. Without overstating the case, the West, and above all Europe, is undergoing such major change at the beginning of the twenty-first century that it is no longer logical to expect the future to be simply an extrapolation and continuation of the recent past. And this could well have far-reaching consequences for architecture.

Of course, this is not the first time that people have declared that things will never be the same again, that the old times will never return. And up to now reality has usually turned out to be much better than the doomsayers predicted. But there are reasons why Europe in particular should consider the possibility that this time it really might turn out differently. Western prosperity and the head start that the wealthy countries have built up over the rest of the world during the past century-and-a-half, are the outcome of a succession of exceptional circumstances, some with roots dating back to the late Middle Ages, but most originating in the eighteenth and nineteenth centuries. And it is first and foremost these economic and demographic circumstances that are now in the process of changing. European countries, which are among the richest in the world, have been hard hit by the economic crisis that began in 2008 (and by the draconian measures their governments deemed necessary in order to remain creditworthy). Even now, the rich countries are still rich, but economic dynamism there is considerably weaker than in emerging countries – from Brazil to Turkey, from China to Angola, from South Africa to India.

After Japan, the European countries have the highest average age and the lowest birth rates. The low growth and even contraction of the economy and the population have obvious consequences for building production and thus for architecture. And the impact is especially hard in Europe which is without doubt the continent with the highest quotient of architecture and architects. Without wishing to fall into rigid determinism, if there are fewer people now and into the future, it stands to reason that there will be less work for all those architects to do.

**Post-era**
Apart from the economic and demographic stagnation that is robbing European (and Japanese) architecture of much of its dynamism, there are the major political and cultural shifts that have been taking place since the 1970s, not just in Europe but in the Western world as a whole. This is far too complex to be simply labelled 'postmodernism', but for convenience's sake that may for the moment be the best word. Postmodernism in this instance refers not to the candy-coloured classicist style in architecture, or to the *citazionismo* in the visual arts, but to the attitude that underlies them and that pervades almost every aspect of postmodernism, from literature to fact-free politics: the cultural relativism of 'anything goes'. Before postmodernism there was modernism, which was based on the industrial idea of growth and progress, of technological modernization, of a development in a particular direction. Postmodernism may at first have seemed like a reaction to modernism, a counter-movement, but the essence of postmodernism turned out to be that everything can go in any direction at all, can exist side by side. As such, postmodernism is a complex form of stagnation, the creation of a worthless vacuum. Postmodernism has been around for quite a while, yet only now is that stagnation becoming obvious. In a review of Hari Kunzru's *Gods Without Men*, published in *The International Herald Tribune*, Douglas Coupland described the twenty-first century as the beginning of

1.
Douglas Coupland, 'Connection across time and space' in: *The International Herald Tribune*, 10/11 March 2012, p. 22.

2.
Kurt Andersen, 'You Say You Want a Devolution?' in: *Vanity Fair*, Jan 2012, pp. 74-82.

an 'aura-free universe in which all eras coexist at once – a state of possibly permanent atemporality given to us courtesy of the Internet. No particular era now dominates. We live in a post-era era without forms of its own powerful enough to brand the times. The zeitgeist of 2012 is that we have a lot of zeit but not much geist. I can't believe I just wrote that last sentence, but it's true.'[1] That same argument had been expounded two months earlier in *Vanity Fair* by Kurt Andersen in 'You Say You Want a Devolution?'. Early on he writes: 'Since 1992, as the technological miracles and wonders have propagated and the political economy has transformed, the world has become radically and profoundly new. …Here is what's odd: during the same 20 years, the appearance of the world (computers, TVs, telephones, and music players aside) has changed hardly at all, less than it did during any 20-year period for at least a century. The past is a foreign country, but the recent past – the 00s, the 90s, even a lot of the 80s – *looks* almost identical to the present.' The article concludes: 'We seem to have trapped ourselves in a vicious cycle – economic progress and innovation stagnated, except in information technology; which leads us to embrace the past and turn the present into a pleasantly eclectic for-profit museum; which deprives the cultures of innovation of the fuel they need to conjure genuinely new ideas and forms; which deters radical change, reinforcing the economic (and political) stagnation. I've been a big believer in historical pendulum swings – American sociopolitical cycles that tend to last, according to historians, about 30 years. So maybe we are coming to the end of this cultural era of the Same Old Same Old. As the baby-boomers who brought about this ice age finally shuffle off, maybe America and the rich world are on the verge of a cascade of the wildly new and insanely great. Or maybe, I worry some days, this is the way that Western civilization declines, not with a bang, but with a long, nostalgic whimper.'[2]

Globalization, which became a frequent topic of conversation in the 1990s, has reduced the differences between here and there because the same phenomena, fashions and trends can be found everywhere. Whether the world is indeed flat, to borrow Thomas Friedman's metaphor, has been disputed with all kinds of arguments, but it is clear that the world view of a great many people is determined by a consciousness or feeling of being connected with the rest of the world. Even without the Internet. The publication of a vast array of books with words like global, globalized and globalization in the title is in itself an indication of this. And even the emergence of the alter-globalization movement, which is opposed to the neo-liberal excesses of globalization, is part of the same phenomenon.
The blurring of the differences between here and there effected by globalization, happened with time in Coupland's 'post-era' condition, with the result that the distinction between today and yesterday has evaporated. Everything is here and now. It is tempting to see the digital revolution as the great equalizer, as the destroyer of distance in time and space. The Internet certainly plays a big role in the experience of this permanent here and now, this lack of difference between centre (here and now) and everything that might be characterized as periphery (there and then). The Internet and globalization have made the world both bigger and smaller, and thanks to the anything goes attitude, many people no longer even care how they see this world, whether as bigger or smaller.
The experience of the effects of globalization has undoubtedly fuelled the relativism of postmodernism, but conversely there is something to be said for the hypothesis that thanks to postmodernism, it is easier to conceive, imagine and experience globalization. What does not belong to today or yesterday is the past, a homogeneous continuum of 'floating coffins, carried

3.
Alessandro Baricco, *I Barbari. Saggio sulla mutazione*, 2006. English translation based on the Dutch edition of this collection of essays, *De Barbaren*, Amsterdam 2010, p. 161.

4.
This essay was originally published in *The National Interest* (Summer 1989) and can be accessed at www.wesjones.com/eoh.htm

along by the current' according to Alessandro Baricco in his book *I Barbari*, first published in 2006. Baricco claimed that for the barbarians, which we ourselves are (or soon will be), 'the past is arranged in a single trajectory that can be defined as "that which no longer exists". Whereas for civilization the repeated measuring of the distance from the past … is the very heart of the matter … for barbarians that distance is always the same. The Greek column, the monocle, the colt and the medieval relic all occupy the same trajectory and are all piled up on the same dumping ground. In a way they are also immediately accessible: there's no need to delve deep, you just stick your hand out and there they are.'[3]

The notion that we have entered a new dimension in which time and space have lost their previous meaning, and that, despite all that has happened, 'our' world in its present form has come to a standstill, can be dismissed as a narcissistic postmodern analysis, but perhaps there is something in it. It also chimes with an idea that emerged in the early 1990s and was made famous by Francis Fukuyama. As early as 1989, even before the Cold War had ended, he argued in his essay 'The End of History' that 'what we may be witnessing is not just the end of the Cold War, or the passing of a particular period of post-war history, but the end of history as such: that is, the end point of mankind's ideological evolution and the universalization of Western liberal democracy as the final form of human government'.[4]

It is indeed an irony of history that Fukuyama should have based his analysis of the fall of communism on the Hegelian view of history, with a beginning, middle and end, which was an article of faith within Marxist theory (Georg Wilhelm Friedrich Hegel himself having placed the end of history in 1806, the year in which Napoleon was defeated).

A similar gist – that the end of the Cold War signalled the end of a period – can be found in a book published

Unfinished building project, Lahinch, Ireland.

two years later by the Marxist historian Eric Hobsbawm, *The Age of Extremes: A History of the World, 1914–1991*. Unlike Fukuyama, Hobsbawm contended that 'the historical forces that shaped the [20th] century, are continuing to operate. We live in a world captured, uprooted and transformed by the titanic economic and techno-scientific process of the development of capitalism, which has dominated the past two or three centuries'. But, he added, 'We know, or at least it is reasonable to suppose, that it cannot go on ad infinitum. The future cannot be a continuation of the past, and there are signs, both externally, and, as it were, internally, that we have reached a point of historical crisis'.[5] According to Hobsbawm, this crisis had already revealed itself in the arts, as is clear from the title of a chapter devoted to post-war art, 'The Avant-garde Dies – The Arts After 1950', in which he assigned postmodernism the role of herald.

5.
Eric Hobsbawm, *The Age of Extremes; A History of the World, 1914–1991*, New York 1995 (orig. London 1994), pp. 584-585.

What does this have to do with architecture? Everything. For there, too, one discerns a similar stagnation, the end of a development. Despite the many differences in nuance, the architecture of 2010 is not substantially different from that of 1990. Not only are the same famous names still famous, but the groove in which architecture finds itself is still that of starchitects, icons, Bilbao effects.

Ghost suburb in Seseña, Spain.

New stars have been added to the architectural firmament, like the latest golden boy, Bjarke Ingels. And everywhere, even in the most unexpected places, the search goes on for recognizable icons (remarkably often museums, those flagships of postmodernist architecture) capable of lending prestige to a place where it is sorely lacking. Take all the comings and goings of plans for new Guggenheim Museums, of which the best-known built exemplar in Spain's Basque Country is just one (see also Guadalajara, Vilnius, Tokio, Rio de Janeiro, Helsinki, Las Vegas and Abu Dhabi), and not even the first. Back in 1989 Hans Hollein won an invited competition for a Guggenheim in Salzburg that was never built.

Looking back over the past 25 years, compared with the 25 years before that, little has changed in architecture. All that has happened is that an awful lot of new architecture has been built, to the extent that even a village with fewer than a thousand inhabitants, like Raiding in Austria, has a concert hall (designed by Atelier Kempe Thill), and a small town like Avilés in Spain (pop. 83,000) can build its own Niemeyer, even if the cultural centre named after its illustrious Brazilian architect had to close after only a few months owing to financial problems.

São Paulo, Brazil

The 2010 BRIC summit, Brasilia, Brazil.

# 2

It is easier to see this moment of stagnation as the end of something, than as the beginning of what is to come. Yet it is equally possible that what now looks like the post-Cold War period may presently turn out to be the beginning of something completely new. The fact that for at least twenty years there has been nothing new under the sun and that there is no clear direction discernible in architectural events (a more appropriate word than 'developments') could be explained using the popular historical metaphor of the pendulum swing. Perhaps the present time is best compared with a very long pendulum swing that goes slower and slower until the maximum amplitude is reached. Or perhaps this is already the moment just after the turning point when the pendulum very gradually begins to pick up speed again.
This idea is broached in an article by Paul Kennedy, 'Crossing a Watershed, Unawares'.[6] Kennedy describes a 'slow buildup of forces for change, mainly invisible, almost always unpredictable, that sooner or later will turn one age into another'. He detects signs of such a build-up: 'The waning of the dollar's heft, the unwinding of European dreams, the arms race in Asia, and the

[6] Paul Kennedy, 'Crossing a Watershed, Unawares' in: *The New York Times*, 25 October 2011.

paralysis of the U.N. Security Council whenever a veto is threatened – do not these, taken together, suggest that we are moving into new, uncharted waters, into a troubled world compared with which the obvious joy of customers emerging from an Apple store with an updated device look, well, of limp and secondary significance?'. Kennedy believes that people in the West currently find themselves in the same position as people over five centuries ago. 'No one alive in 1480 would recognize the world of 1530.' This, according to Kennedy, is our '1480'. While Kennedy sees a shift in the centre of gravity from West to East, from the Atlantic Ocean to the Pacific, there are also perceptible shifts from North to South, from rich to formerly poor. Most economic forecasts locate a large part of global economic growth for the coming twenty years in the southern hemisphere and above all in places that were seldom a source of good news during the twentieth century. In an article in the April 2012 issue of the African edition of Forbes, whose very existence is an indication of changing relationships, African stock markets ('outperforming those of many developed countries') were dubbed the continent's 'best kept secret'. The fact that Portuguese citizens are emigrating to Angola in search of work and that Angola is investing in the economy of the old colonial ruler, which must privatize struggling state-owned firms under the terms of an €80bn International Monetary Fund bailout of 2011, speaks volumes. And Africa, more than any other part of the world, is where China is manifesting itself and, in exchange for the construction of infrastructure, securing its own future demand for raw materials and food.

### Hegemony
Kennedy's 1480 comparison is well chosen, because in the period when the West started to conquer the world lies the origin of that world hegemony, initially European, then Western and in the past century primarily American,

Istanbul, Turkey.

which is now drawing to a close. Of course, this is not the first time that the decline of the West has been foretold – first it was Japan that would take over the reins, then it looked like being the Asian Tigers, and now it's China and India. You don't hear anyone talking about Japan as an economic superpower any more. Nowadays it is the colossal national debt, the years of deflation and stagnation and the rapid ageing of its population (the median age is already above 44) that dominate the news reports. Thus whether it will be China and India, or one of the other upcoming BRICS (which bizarrely includes an economically, politically, socially and demographically challenged Russia) or some other nation altogether that will assume power, is still an open question. But that European hegemony, which some would claim ended with the First World War, is continuing to decline is undeniable.
This does not necessarily manifest itself in a substantial decrease in prosperity at the macro level, although the number of poor inhabitants of wealthy countries is shamefully high. Within the EU, almost a quarter of the population lives below the poverty line, defined as 60 per cent of the average wage, in the US one-sixth of the population lives below a poverty line set considerably lower at an income of $22,314 a year for a family of four (45% of the

Doha, Qatar.

average family income) and $11,139 for a single person. Yet despite this and the protracted recession, the inhabitants of rich countries are and remain much, much wealthier than the almost three billion people with less than two dollars a day to live on.
In that respect, the division of the world into developed and undeveloped countries, the only transition between them a small number of emerging countries, still adheres to the broad outlines of the world order laid down in 1500, with Europe and later also the New World on one side, and on the other the colonies and conquered territories.

**Revolutions**
Europe's hegemony was perpetuated by a succession of interrelated revolutions: scientific, agrarian, industrial and demographic. The first three formed the basis for the modernity of Western society, for capitalism (and communism), for civil, democratic society and so on and so forth. The final revolution is the demographic, which refers to the spectacular growth in population, from 136 million in 1750, to 265 million in 1850, to 410 million in 1900, such that at the beginning of the twentieth century, almost twenty-five per cent of the world population was European. That percentage has since halved.

In light of these revolutions, it could also be argued that the pendulum, which is now close to its maximum amplitude, takes less than five centuries for one full swing. Half as long for example, because there is a lot to be said for the argument that Europe is now experiencing the end of the revolutions that began to take shape from 1750 onwards. Or perhaps there are two pendulums that just for a moment are moving (or standing still) in synchrony.

The pendulum movement that began around 1750, is directly related to the Industrial Revolution, which in many places is manifestly at an end. The sublime post-industrial landscapes in Europe and the US are the visible remnants. De-industrialization began in many countries way back in the 1960s and '70s, but the disruptive effects only started to make themselves felt much later. The industrial powerhouses of national economies have in many cases become the poorest areas in the country, now that productive capitalism has been far outstripped in scale and importance by financial capitalism.

'Better belching smokestacks than the bubbles of financial capitalism' ran the title of an opinion piece by Frank Ankersmit, Emeritus Professor of Intellectual History at Groningen University, published in the Dutch broadsheet *NRC Handelsblad* in October 2011. 'The money generated by financial capitalism always ends up in bubbles – housing bubbles, dot-com bubbles, stock market bubbles, commodity bubbles and all the rest. Where else could it go, other than in even bigger banking giants or even higher bonuses. That doesn't really amount to much. Conversely, the money generated by industrial capitalism is invested in the companies where that money was earned – as it should be. Sooner or later bubbles always burst and in so doing destabilize the economic order. Company investments are however generally the basis for a healthy and stable economy.'[7]

7.
Frank Ankersmit, 'Liever rokende schoorstenen dan de bubbels van het financiële kapitalisme' in: *NRC Handelsblad*, 8 October 2011.

Leaving aside for the moment the fact that belching smokestacks are a symbol not only of a stable economy, but also of exploitation and greed, Ankersmit's distinction between industrial and financial capitalism mirrors, in all simplicity, the reality that it is easier to make money with money (and to destroy money with money), than with the production of goods, the basis of industrial capitalism.

**Bubbles**
Financial capitalism can be seen as the last frontier of the capitalism that grew out of the Industrial Age. After all the innovations in the field of production of goods, transport, communications and automation, where money was the essential lubricant for achieving a goal, the lubricant itself has become the goal, generating ever more implausible bubbles, although every real estate bubble is actually disarmingly straightforward because it still involves a concrete product or the prospect of one. There is a direct line running from the dot-com bubble to the financial crisis of 2008, for both of them turned the motto 'first see, then believe' on its head: first believe, then you may perhaps see. It is not the concrete product or service that determines the value, but the idea for a product or a service. An optimistic representation of a heavily loss-making idea is all that is needed to be able to sell it for a lot of money or to float it on the stock market. The accumulation of favourable prospect upon favourable prospect is typical of the upward spiral of every bubble, from tulipomania to the sub-prime CDOs, and in retrospect every bubble can be seen to have a lot in common with a pyramid scheme, which is governed not by the conventional relation between demand and supply, but by a constant acceleration of demand based on nothing more than the demand itself. Until the pyramid collapses.
Without wishing to get into the naming and blaming game, if statues were to be erected in the name of

Remnant of the Occupy camp in Washington (DC), USA.

financial capitalism, they would have to be of the strongest advocates and most vigorous implementers of the 'free market': Ronald Reagan and Margaret Thatcher. They were the founders of an ideology that their political successors, whether Conservative and Republican or Labour and Democratic, continued to develop. The deregulation of the financial markets, in the UK ushered in by the Big Bang of 1986, and in the US by the gradual repeal of the New Deal era's Glass-Steggall Act, opened the way for financial engineering unequalled in the history of capitalism, in which architecture, to the extent that it still had a role, was usually no more than a security whose main function was to maximize the leverage on increasingly obscure financial constructions, of which the CDO of sub-prime mortgage-backed bonds was just one example.
Deregulation infected almost every area of society, up to and including old utilities like water and power. It goes without saying that architecture did not escape either. European directives on competition and tendering are based on the idea of a level playing field, but here too what was intended to create a free market, resulted in a deep divide between on the one hand a Champions League of big firms which, because they are big, are virtually the only ones able to compete

for big projects and in so doing remain big. And on the other hand, the rest (another instance of the now common division between one and 99 per cent). It is a paradox of the free market that in every sector a small number of big players, be they called Google or Nestlé, come out on top with a disproportionate market share, so that the end result of super capitalism sometimes looks insidiously like the state monopolies in socialist countries.

**Surf capitalism**
Financial capitalism is a sign of this postmodernist era, something Alessandro Baricco also points out in *I Barbari*. Freeloading is more profitable than doing something oneself. Take a company like Google, which doesn't produce a scintilla of information itself, and doesn't earn anything from the search machine either, but makes a fortune out of advertisements related to the search machine. Under industrial capitalism you would have had to pay for a search request, under today's capitalism it is free and the money is earned elsewhere. Facebook makes money by exploiting the wealth of personal and intimate details that people freely (in both senses of the word) place on their Facebook page. Both companies leave production, of information and of trivial details from people's private lives (which are individually worthless but turn out to be valuable when added together), to others.
This is no blazing critique of this kind of 'surf capitalism', which exists and is not going to disappear any time soon, but a simple observation. A similarly simple observation is that the construction of a building, the realization of a project, is caught between these two forms of capitalism.
Architecture is first and foremost linked to the belching smokestacks. It belongs to production capitalism.
In its current form, architecture is still a product of the

Industrial Age, as is the idea that underpins it, namely that every change is an improvement (no profession is so imbued with the soap powder advertising optimism of 'now better than ever'). But buildings also belong to the category of products on which financial capitalism thrived. Just as the millions of (unpaid) Facebook users ensure that Mark Zuckerberg is on his way to becoming the richest man in the universe, so all the (in this case paid) parties who make buildings, starting with architects, ensure that those who own the buildings become wealthier from it. At least, that's how things worked until the recession. Because construction alone will not make you seriously rich. According to the United Nations Environment Programme (UNEP), the construction industry in the European Union is the 'largest industrial sector, contributing approximately 11% to GNP, with more than 25 million people directly and indirectly involved'.[8] Twenty-five million people is upwards of thirteen per cent of the EU workforce, an indication of how labour-intensive construction is, and of how much effort it takes to earn money with construction. There is – or rather was, until property prices started to plunge – much more to be earned with the end result of all those efforts. Willmott Dixon, a major British developer, came to the conclusion that 'half of all fixed capital formation annually is vested in buildings, which, taken together with the inherited assets of buildings, represents about 75 per cent of all UK wealth'.[9]

A large part of the value of a building resides not in the bricks and mortar, but in the land. In the Netherlands, for example, agricultural land costs a few euros per square metre, less than the cheapest carpet from the lowest priced discounter. When that land is zoned for development, it can suddenly be worth a hundred times that amount. People buying into new-build projects must pay the residual land value, with the local council and developer sharing the increase in value. Thus the

8.
www.unep.or.jp/ietc/focus/Energy Cities1.asp

9.
Briefing Note 33: 'The Impacts of Construction and the Built Environment', December 2010, produced by WD Re-Thinking Ltd.

developer doesn't greatly care that the actual construction will not earn much, while the council simply profits from the allocation of land.

While every new car loses ten per cent of its value as soon as it leaves the showroom, with house prices the reverse is the case. In a lot of countries house prices rise faster than wages and inflation. Everyone accepts that a car is written off after ten years, but that a house might also drop in value simply does not enter the minds of private home owners. A house is an investment that is supposed to appreciate in value over time.

**Balance sheets**
Institutional parties in housing construction on the other hand most certainly employ the accounting principles of depreciation, as do investors in office buildings and shopping centres, who are equally dogmatic on this point. Housing associations generally employ a forty-year depreciation period, which means that one day later the value is zero and demolition is no longer – from an accounting perspective, at least – destruction of capital. For office buildings the lifespan is often even shorter. At the beginning of 2012, real estate adviser DTZ Zadelhoff not only advised investors to write off ten billion euros on empty office buildings in the Netherlands (where one-sixth of the 48 million square metres of total office space are empty), but also suggested they adopt a new rule of thumb for offices: every ten years a complete interior refurbishment and every twenty years a makeover of both interior and exterior.

Real estate is in certain respects part of financial capitalism, but there is one important difference. You cannot go short on property. From falls in prices, such as in Ireland where the value of commercial property plunged sixty per cent and rents were halved, nobody profits excepts the renter. (Although it's not impossible that at one of the Goldman Sachses of this world someone will conjure up a clever wheeze for profiting from this as well.) In the wake of the massive evaporation of capital in the financial crisis the banks are concentrating on improving their balance sheets and depositing their money with the European Central Bank, rather than lending it to, say, developers (who would in any case be well advised to refrain from adding to vacancy levels). In addition, investors are less inclined to put their money into buildings because they must first swallow the bitter pill of writing off their – in part vacant – real estate property, which is worth less than its current balance sheet value. That balance sheet value is another reason why a lot of vacant real estate is not being converted, because after the renovation it has to be revalued and the value under the new market conditions often turns out to be considerably lower than the old book value, which translates into a lower leverage. Because the banks are not keen to lend money (to any sector, not just construction), the general economic rebound is faltering and there is even less incentive to build.

## Surplus

One aspect of the recession in the construction industry is the recurrent hog cycle. While over- and under-production are inherent to the slowness with which the sector adapts to changing economic circumstances, this time the mismatch between demand and supply is especially big, for both houses and offices. Moreover, there are a lot of companies that because of continuing contracts are more spaciously housed than they would wish with their now reduced workforce. So the actual surplus is much greater.

Architectural firms are now having to contend with a similar Potemkin effect, which is all the more remarkable after the growth that many firms experienced in step with the financial and real estate bubbles. The facade of the office and the website is still impressive, but the

10.
The Architects' Council of Europe, 'Ninth Snapshot Survey of the Impact of Economic Downturn', January 2012, www.ace-cae.eu

space behind is sometimes depressingly empty. Many European architects have lost a large part of their work, their turnover, their personnel and their clients and are diligently searching for a way out in the form of a specialization (sustainability), a new work sphere (China), a niche (conversion) or a new role (as spatial social worker, a bit like in the 1970s). Or in a few cases they manage to keep the facade in place by engaging young staff members on a paltry salary, in an endlessly long internship. At the beginning of 2012, in the ninth of the three-monthly surveys carried out by the Architects' Council of Europe, over 51 per cent of surveyed architects described their situation as bad or very bad.[10]

The poor market for construction is not just an economic story, for with a few simple sums it is possible to foresee that the demographic transition from growth to shrinkage, which is already under way in Europe and Japan, and which awaits China with its one-child policy from 2040, will further erode the foundations of the industrial system of growth and progress. Even if the tendency for families to become ever smaller were to continue indefinitely until finally everyone is a singleton, there would still be less need for new construction than in periods of population growth. Moreover, as the population ages and shrinks, so the ratio of employed to retired people shifts. At present the ratio is four to one in Europe, before long it will be two to one. Pension funds will have to start paying out more and will have less to invest, which is a double brake on the real estate market. Less is needed and there is less money available to invest in, say, office buildings. The demographic dividend Europe has profited from since the nineteenth century with its expanding population, and of which the post-1945 baby boom in the West was the final peak, is now turning into its opposite. Sticking to financial terms: what comes next is a demographic margin call.

Singapore.

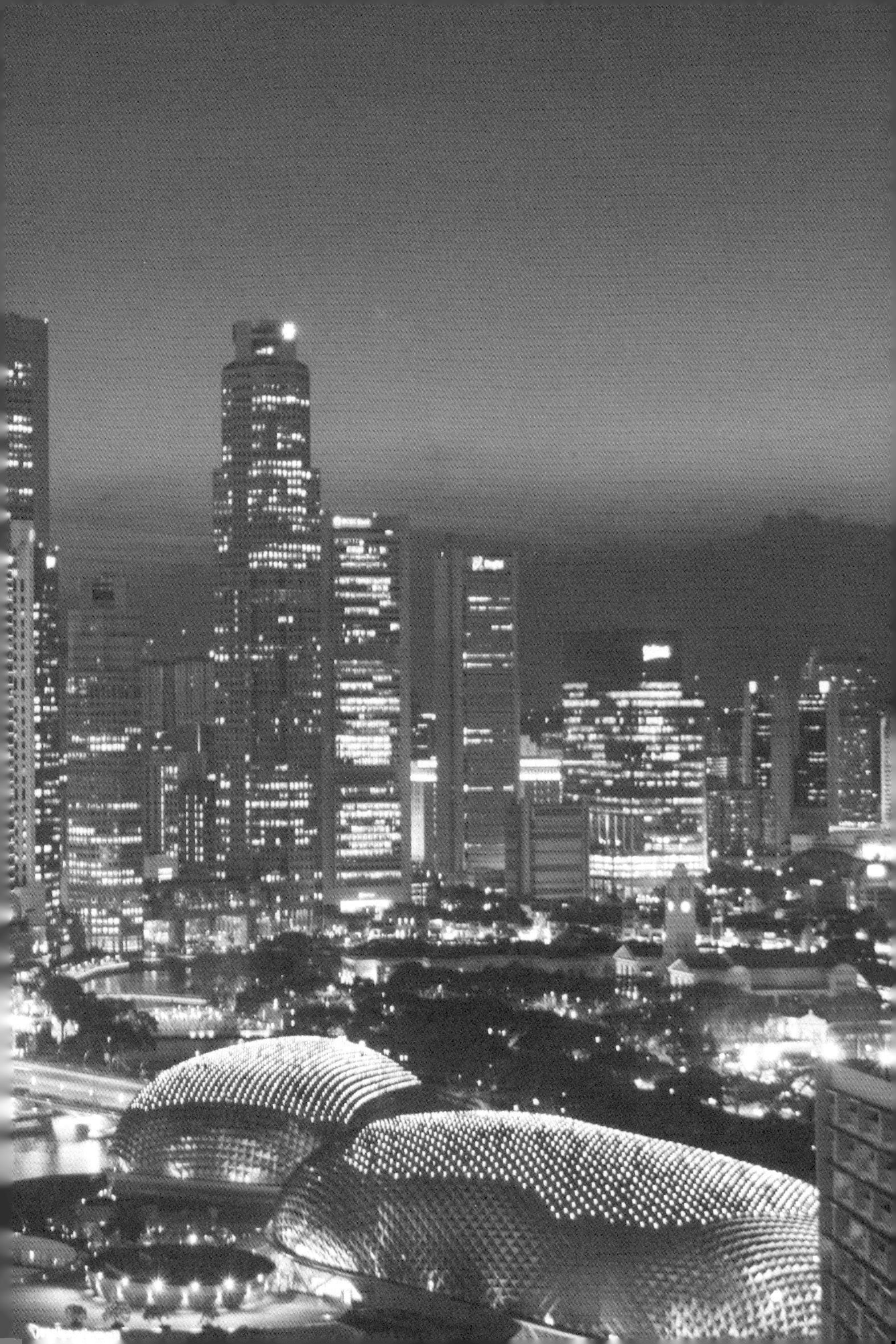

The 2010 Asia-Pacific Economic Cooperation summit, Yokohama, Japan.

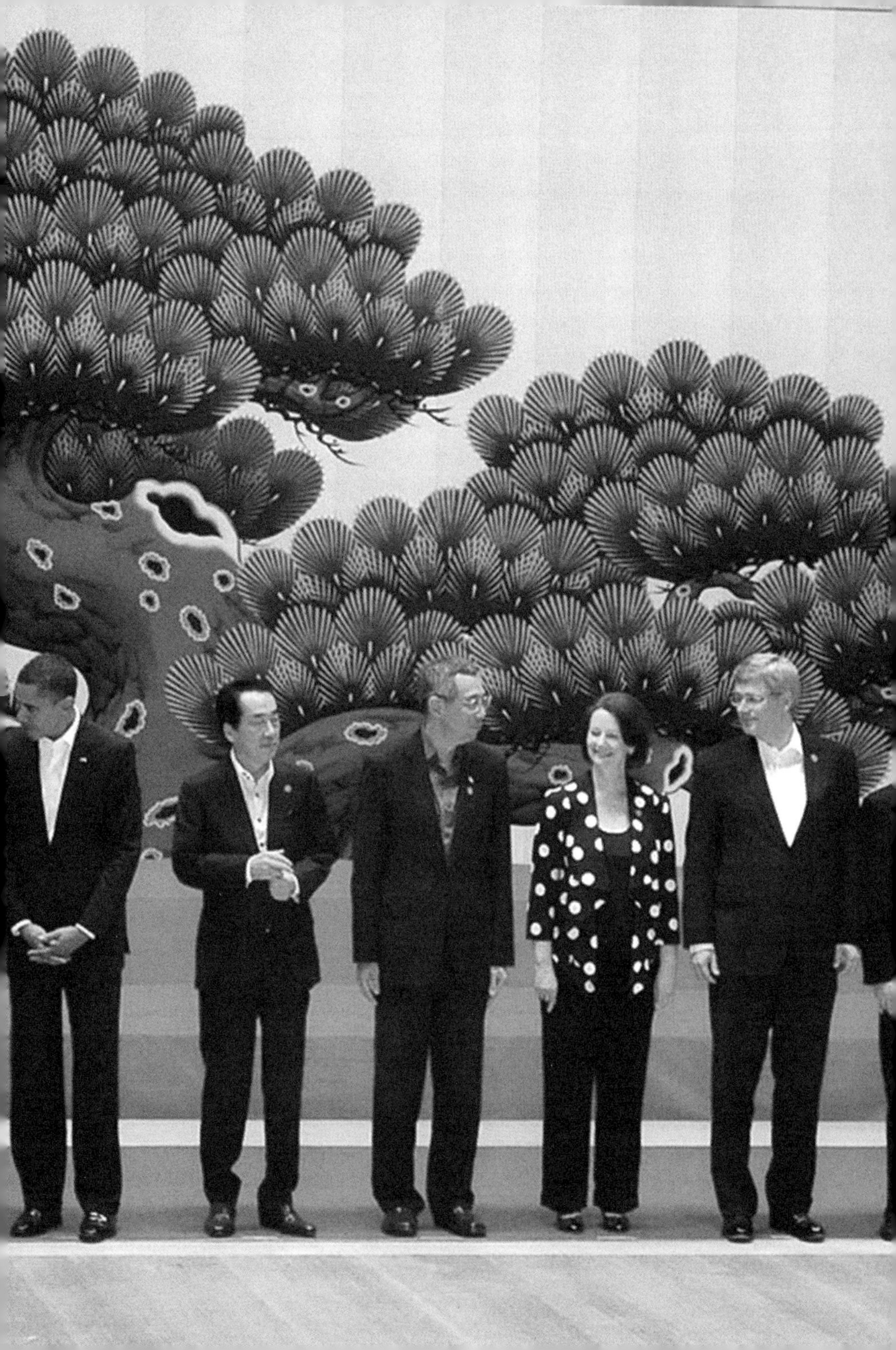

# 3

Architecture follows the money. No money, no buildings (let alone details). Money does not always and everywhere lead to architecture. But architecture is like an index fossil of capital: where there is a lot of architecture, there is also a lot of money and the economy grows (to which everything that is built and increases in value also contributes). Look at Ireland, where the economy grew by an average of ten per cent per annum between 1995 and 2000, and thereafter, until the hard landing in 2008, continued to grow at an average of over five per cent per annum. The prosperity also manifested itself in architecture. Before 1995 exceptional new architecture was rare, today once again very little new architecture is being built. One of the most noteworthy post-crash projects in Ireland is Dominic Stevens' almost no-budget self-build house which cost only 25,000 euros and that anyone can make using the detailed, step-by-step instructions he has posted on his Irish Vernacular website.[11]

The same applies to the Netherlands where the heyday of Superdutch coincided with the economic boom of the 1990s, a blossoming that, following a dip shortly after the turn of the century, persisted until the recession commenced in 2008. And to Spain which, from the 1990s, courtesy of the European Structural Funds, experienced huge economic development and acquired a great deal of new architecture into the bargain. In Spain and the Netherlands the GDP tripled in twenty years; in Ireland in the same period it increased by four hundred per cent.[12] The connection between peaks in architecture and peaks

11.
www.irishvernacular.com/step-by-step.html

12.
www.economywatch.com

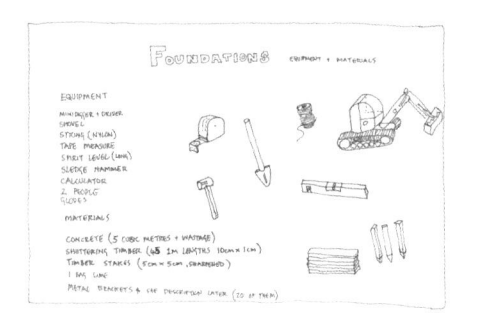

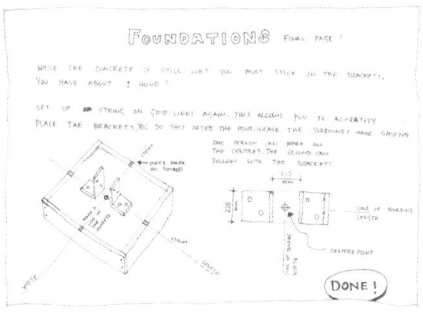

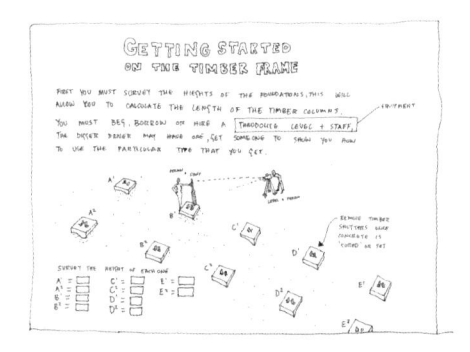

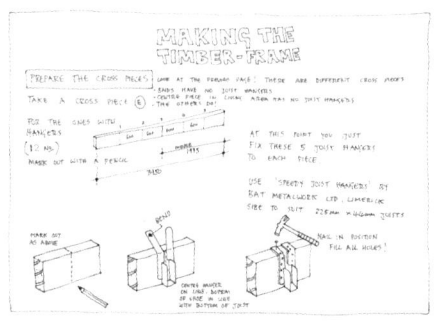

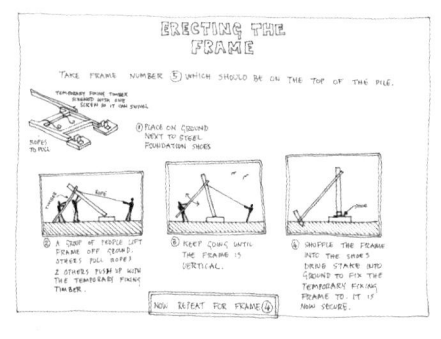

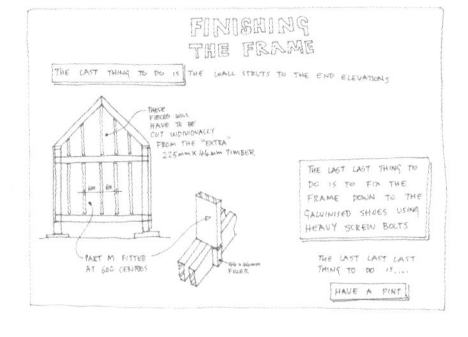

Dominic Stevens, Manual for a
low cost, self-build house, 2011.

in economic conditions is also evident in the so-called skyscraper index. Time and again, projects with a record height – Chrysler, Empire State, Sears, Petronas – have turned out to be a harbinger of an economic downturn. (Which really makes one wonder why the mere drawing up of such plans should not be an immediate reason for aborting them.) The current record holder, the 828-metre Burj Khalifa in Dubai, also belongs to this category. At this height the law of diminishing returns applies in spades. Because of all the structure required, the top floors yield a mere sixty per cent net floor area.

Until a few hours before the opening on 4 January 2010, the tower was called Burj Dubai, but at the last minute it was renamed in honour of the president of the Emirates, Khalifa bin Zayed Al Nahayan. The president is also the Emir of Abu Dhabi, which a month earlier had helped its neighbouring emirate Dubai to pay off part of the 59 billion dollar debt that the emirate's investment arm, Dubai World, had accumulated with investments in its own country and in projects like MGM Grand Casino in Las Vegas.

The price per square metre in Burj Kahlifa in 2012 was just a quarter of the pre-crash peak in 2008. Architecture in times of prosperity is not only an object of speculation, but also leads to a proliferation of a genre of buildings that are speculative, in the sense that they are premised on an increase in value. Why else would anyone be willing to pay over twenty thousand euros per square metre for a dwelling in what would briefly become the tallest building in the world, in a city that is as yet little more than a promise of urbanity? This is architecture that does not arise out of any immediate social demand or need, but which speculates on its possible attraction for consumers, buyers, tenants in a place that may possibly become attractive because everything there is in the superlative. (Burj Khalifa's chief merit is that it is so tall.) Utopias were discredited after (and because of) modernism and are nowadays easily dismissed as ideological chimeras;

13.
www.creditloan.com, based on information from money.ca.msn.com

14.
John Hannigan, *Fantasy City: Pleasure and Profit in the Postmdern Metropolis*, London 1998: Howard Berkes, *Olympic Caveats: Host Cities Risk Debt, Scandal*, 1 October 2009, www.npr.org

what has replaced them, as in Dubai, is in fact every bit as utopian, albeit based on an ideal devoid of any ideals that go deeper than the desire for a perfectly functioning free market. Modernism's social ideal that everyone will have it better, is replaced here by a purely financial justification, that everyone will do better out of it.

## Top ten

Dubai World's willingness to invest in a casino is revealing. Equally revealing is Creditloan.com's list of the ten most expensive buildings, which includes Burj Khalifa. The costs of these ten buildings, the earliest of which was completed in 1990 and the most recent in 2010, range from just under a billion to 2.7 billion dollars (although it is unclear whether and how differences in price levels between 1990 and 2010 have been factored in). The top ten include three casinos in Las Vegas (Mandalay Bay, Bellagio and Wynn Las Vegas), two financial institutions in China, the Bank of China in Hongkong and Shanghai's World Financial Centre, two sports buildings, the new stadium of the New York Yankees (a club with a debt in the order of two billion dollars), and the new Wembley Stadium in London, two mega towers, the Burj Khalifa in Dubai and the Taipei 101 in Taiwan (one of the few high-rise projects that did not presage a crisis). Plus an exceptional residential building, the Antilia Residence in Mumbai.[13]

Although Western countries fill half of the top ten places, even in the case of number one (Wynn Las Vegas) it is with buildings that house functions that have no immediate social relevance, let alone be called indispensable. Casinos are at best metaphors for the current financial capitalism. Big sporting clubs, contrary to what the clubs would repeatedly have us believe, have little or no positive impact on urban or national economies.[14] That five of the ten most expensive buildings are not in the West, and that of the five that are, only one is in Europe – in the country that since Margaret Thatcher has been the

SOM, Burj Khalifa, Dubai,
United Arab Emirates, 2010.

Butler Ashworth Architects, with The Jerde
Partnership, Wynn Las Vegas casino and
resort, Las Vegas, Nevada, USA, 2005.

C.Y. Lee & Partners, Taipei 101,
Taipei, Taiwan, 2004.

Perkins & Will, Antilia Residence,
Mumbai, India, 2010.

European bastion of Anglo-Saxon neo-liberalism – is a sign of the shifting balance, both economic and cultural. Architecture is strongly tied up with European notions which, thanks to European hegemony, have been propagated and perpetuated worldwide. Take a look at any overview of architectural history: it is mainly about Europe. The definition of architecture is in most cases implicitly determined by what architecture in Europe became after 1750: the work of professionals, who approach the built environment with cultural ambitions, and to a large extent work on behalf of government and society. Before then, architecture was something that only the monarch, church and merchant could afford. After 1750 architecture throughout Europe became of and for everyone, it became an omnipresent, all-encompassing and integral part of civil society. In other parts of the world that was never the case to the same degree, and nor is it today, not even in North America or Australia.

Architecture may look the same everywhere but it does not have the same cultural and social significance, if it has them at all, as in Europe. If the ten most expensive buildings in the world are an indication of what is happening in architecture, then Europe is no longer even playing second fiddle. And the public and cultural dimension that was so important in Europe from 1750 onwards, scarcely matters at the global level.

Western and modern are two concepts that for a long while overlapped. That overlap continues to make itself felt in the way that modernity and modernization are largely understood in terms of Western, Enlightenment-derived notions, and in the difficulty of truly understanding modernization in countries like China, India, Singapore or Qatar from a Western perspective.

The conceptual framework originating from the revolutions that from the eighteenth century onwards shaped the modern West – Europe and the European-conquered New World – was imposed on a large part of the world during the period of Western world hegemony. This is a point raised by Dipesh Chakrabarty in *Provincializing Europe*: 'Concepts such as citizenship, the state, civil society, public sphere, human rights, equality before the law, the individual, distinctions between public and private, the idea of the subject, democracy, popular sovereignty, social justice, scientific rationality, and so on all bear the burden of European thought and history'.[15] But now it turns out that what appeared to be universal, is not. And that is equally true of the architecture that was built on the foundation of these Western notions. From a Western perspective, globalization seemed to result chiefly in a dissemination and acceptance of Western phenomena, from McDonald's to democracy to postmodernist architecture. The main objection raised against this globalization was that thanks to the likes of Starbucks and IKEA, everywhere became the same. Much as Coca Cola had for decades been a symbol of the Americanization of the world. But for the rest globalization appeared to be quite enjoyable, especially when the putative 'new economy' and the Digital Age arrived and everybody could imagine themselves at the centre of the world and could go everywhere. This happy globalization suffered a heavy blow when it turned out that anti-Western terrorism was equally footloose, and could pop up anywhere.

The high spirits of the optimistic 1990s gave way to the pessimism and fearfulness of the early years of the new century, and now another mood seems to have taken hold: that globalization is not the Westernization of the world, but the other way around. The West is being taken over by the rest of the world.

Eight of the ten most expensive buildings in the world stand in surroundings where the supposedly universal social and civic values are not dominant: in Las Vegas, in the India of Chakrabarty, in countries where democracy is imperfect, such as Taiwan, or absent, such as China and Dubai. Obviously, these most expensive buildings

**15.**
Dipesh Chakrabarty, *Provincializing Europe: Postcolonial Thought and Historical Difference*, Princeton, Oxford 2007, p. 5.

can be designated architecture, but they are not the direct or indirect product of the civil society in the way that European architecture is.

## Flash

The cultural dimension is also under pressure in another way in this Digital Age, in the speed with which architecture as image is disseminated (what holds for all the other media also holds for architectural media). The latest rendering programs have also spawned a fast architecture that is ready to be presented to the world in beautiful, friction-free images even before it has been properly thought out. Compared with the financial world, architecture is always extremely slow. Construction takes so much time that bull-market dream projects can easily turn into nightmares in the subsequent bear market. The turnover rate of architectural images is now exceptionally high, however, thanks to globalization and the new media. The (transient) flashing images seldom show a project in its entirety, from concept to detail. This flash architecture is to construction what high-frequency trading is to the transactions of a jobber sitting in a stock exchange with a telephone clamped to either ear. They comprise their own reality. In flash architecture the creativity, time and effort that have been poured into it are compressed into a few images that briefly reverberate on all the international websites only to make way for the images of the next project, which then enjoys a few hours 'at the top of the list'. The visual culture that has dominated architectural culture since postmodernism is thereby accelerated and architects, willingly or not, become less and less structural engineers and more and more engineers of images and fantasies, in other words what in the world of Disney are known as 'imagineers'. On the Internet, the ever-burgeoning volume of these architectural images constitutes a visual plastic soup that permanently pollutes the digital information oceans.

Shanghai, China.

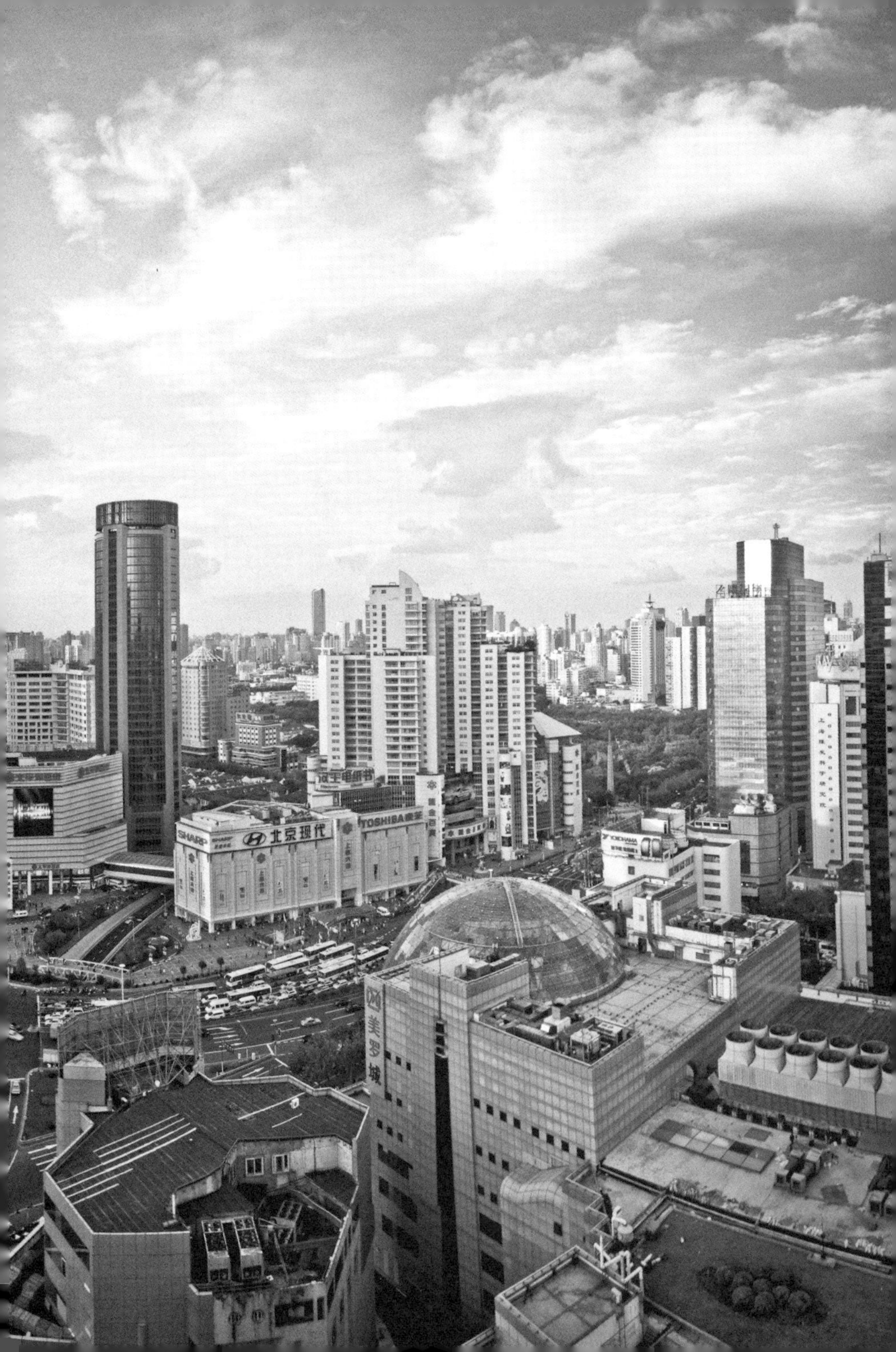
SHARP
北京现代
TOSHIBA
美罗城

The 2011 G20 summit, Cannes, France.

2011

UVELLES IDÉES

# 4

One aspect of globalization is the increased awareness of the existence of global ecological issues, such as climate change and the associated weather weirding, food production, water management, environmental pollution and the depletion of fossil fuels and other raw materials. These problems affect everyone on our planet but it is the rich part of the world, with the biggest ecological footprint, that has a great responsibility for finding solutions for them. Especially since the effects of this crisis are not evenly distributed. A poverty-stricken country like Bangladesh suffers more from a rising sea level than wealthy Switzerland sitting high and dry in the Alps. Worldwide ecological issues have a direct bearing on architecture simply because life (especially in rich countries, and especially in cooler regions) largely takes place indoors, in buildings. A few years back, the American Environmental Protection Agency estimated that 'on average, Americans spend about 90 percent or more of their time indoors'. In other wealthy countries, too, most people will spend the major part of their time indoors, which – by the by – throws a fascinating light on the huge creative and financial efforts to create attractive public outdoor spaces, given that most people will only ever spend a fraction of their time there.

16.
www.epa.gov/
greenbuilding/
pubs/gbstats.pdf,
*Buildings and their Impact on the Environment: A Statistical Summary*, April 2009.

17.
www.unep.or.jp/
ietc/focus/
EnergyCities1.asp

18.
Briefing Note 33: 'The Impacts of Construction and the Built Environment', December 2010, produced by WD Re-Thinking Ltd.

19.
www.unep.or.jp/
ietc/focus/Energy
Cities1.asp

Buildings account for almost forty per cent of total US energy consumption (2005), 72 per cent of total US electricity consumption (2006), 13 per cent of the total water consumed per day in the United States (1995) and almost forty per cent of the nation's total carbon emissions (2008).[16] If one assumes percentages of the same order elsewhere in the rich world, this means that less than half of the environmental impact of wealthy societies can be traced to buildings, whereas people spend virtually their entire lives there. This may appear to put things into a more reassuring perspective, but one must not forget that on top of the environmental impact of the use of buildings, their construction, renovation and demolition also require energy, consume raw materials, and generate $CO_2$ and waste. According to the United Nations Environment Programme (UNEP), in 1999 construction activities contributed to 'over 35% of total global $CO_2$ emissions – more than any other industrial activity'.[17]

In the report 'The Impacts of Construction and the Built Environment' by the Willmott Dixon Group, it is estimated that in the UK 'construction consumes about 4.5% of the national total' of all energy (including transport and embodied energy) and 'around half of all non-renewable resources mankind consumes are used in construction, making it one of the least sustainable industries in the world'.[18] Moreover, according to UNEP, even with the efforts of some developers – like Willmott Dixon – not to produce any more landfill waste, 'the construction sector as a whole is responsible for approximately 40% of all human-produced wastes'.[19] In that respect there is also a positive aspect to the economic trough in which the building industry in Europe finds itself at the moment: the less that is built, the better for the environment. The ecological sense of guilt that has started to make itself felt in the construction industry in recent years is coupled with clever entrepreneurship, for in these times of crisis it turns out that sustainability is just about the last remaining valid argument for legitimizing new construction. In addition, a whole new world of certification and classification has arisen in which, as in the world of boxing, competing organizations award their own titles to champions in every weight division. Just about any building can consequently be declared 'most sustainable' in its own particular category. Up to now these sustainability championships have been won on the building services, and are seldom if ever attributable to the architect. The role of architecture, and of the architect, in this inflationary sustainable construction is in most cases very limited at present.

## Marginal position

Construction and architecture are most certainly not necessarily the same. It has been estimated that approximately 95 per cent of buildings worldwide were built without any input from an architect.[20] In Europe (and probably in Europe alone), the percentage of architecture with architects is substantially higher. That has everything to do with the role and responsibility architects acquired in the nineteenth century when they were entrusted with shaping civil society. The responsibility for shaping society was subsequently expanded by the profession until it finally encompassed the design of the entire world, from sofa cushions to the city. Nowhere is the proportion of do-gooders as high as among Western architects. But given an involvement in no more than five per cent of the built environment, architects do not have the power at a global level to exert genuine influence. Even in Europe the role of the architect is limited, and deregulation has only served to limit it still further. As a result, the position of the European architect is less exceptional than it used to be, and is fast becoming as marginal as in the rest of the world. Because more and more in Europe, as in for example China, all that is

20.
Marcel Vellinga, Paul Oliver and Alexander Bridge, *Atlas of Vernacular Architecture of the World*, London 2008.

David Falconer/NARA, Unlighted business sign during the 1973 fuel crisis, USA.

expected from an architect is a sketch or a preliminary design, which can act as a lever or springboard to get the project off the ground, a project in which both the architect and architecture are soon regarded as *quantités négligeables*. This marginal position is incompatible with the self-image of the architect as all-rounder whose activities will, if not deliver a better world, make the world a better place.

Something else that is alien to the habitude of the architect is the sombre mood that in recent years has taken hold of a large part of the rich world and Europe in particular. Ecological disaster, economic doldrums, the geopolitical decline of the West, the end of the Industrial Age, demographic shrinkage, cultural stagnation: architecture is not the only discipline affected. But for architects, who regard themselves as generalist problem-solvers, the current issues are especially confronting, firstly because there are no easy ways out (such as solving every problem through growth and progress) and secondly because architecture is frequently part of the problem, particularly when it concerns the economy and ecology.
The sombre prospects sketched by the authors of *Limits to Growth*, first published in 1972, just before the First Oil Crisis – the previous boom in future-pessimism – had not

become any less sombre in the 30-year update published in 2004.[21] The idea of overshoot, of exceeding our ecological footprint, of Peak Oil and the depletion of other natural resources, can be found in any number of publications, all variations on a theme that is neatly summarized in the title of Richard Heinberg's book, *Peak Everything: Waking Up to the Century of Decline in the Earth's Resources*.[22]

## Decline

The ecological shifts, including the demographic one, are undoubtedly more far-reaching than the economic problems of the present moment. Even if the economic crisis in the West were to persist for a long time, its effect would be more short-lived and superficial than the ecological consequences of climate change, the depletion of natural resources, the decline in biodiversity, the issue of food production and the pollution of land, air and water. Furthermore, the economic problems in the wealthy West, however great they may be, and however painful at an individual level, from a global perspective are still luxury problems. The US and the EU, which together account for only ten per cent of the world population, have forty per cent of the world's gross domestic product. For the moment, the West is suffering more from the psychology of loss aversion than from loss itself. Yet there is no denying that the sense that the West is in decline is – rightly or wrongly – stronger than ever.

In the shadow of the economic crisis, doomsayers find it easier to be proved right on this point than optimists, especially when valid objections by optimists can be met with 'decline isn't a quick process, nor is it a linear one. Civilizations fall in a stepwise fashion, with periods of crisis and contraction followed by periods of stability and partial recovery'.[23]

Declinism, like decline itself, is not a quick process. What Paul Valéry wrote shortly after the First World War

21.
Donella Meadows, Jorgen Randers, Dennis Meadows, *Limits to Growth: The 30-Year Update*, London/Washington 2010 (2004).

22.
Richard Heinberg, *Peak Everything: Waking Up to the Century of Decline in the Earth's Resources*, Forest Row 2007.

23.
John Michael Greer, *The Long Descent: A User's Guide to the End of the Industrial Age*, Gabriola Island 2008, p. 158.

**24.**
Paul Valéry, 'The Crisis of Mind' in: *The Athenaeum*, April 11 and May 2, 1919; Dambisa Moyo, *How the West Was Lost; Fifty Years of Economic Folly – And the Stark Choices Ahead*, London 2012 (2011).

**25.**
Joseph A. Tainter, *The Collapse of Complex Societies*, Cambridge 2011 (1988), p. 211.

**26.**
Joseph A. Tainter, *The Collapse of Complex Societies*, Cambridge 2011 (1988), p. 215–6.

in 'The Crisis of the Mind', is *mutatis mutandis* not all that different from what Dambisa Moyo contentiously asserted almost a century later in *How the West was Lost*.[24] And the lament that the role of the architect is getting ever smaller compared with an unspecified past, is nothing new. In that respect, decline arguments have long suffered from a diminishing return.

## Collapse

Diminishing return is a phenomenon that anthropologist Joseph A. Tainter described in *The Collapse of Complex Societies* as the crucial factor in every collapse. In brief: at a given moment the costs of maintaining a complex system are higher than the returns. Tainter saw, way before the digital revolution manifested itself to its full extent, and before the big bubbles of the 1990s and 2000s, indications that 'patterns of declining marginal returns can be observed in at least some contemporary industrial societies' in areas such as agriculture, education, management and productivity.[25] At the end of the 1980s Tainter was writing that 'it is difficult to know whether world industrial society has yet reached the point where the marginal return for its overall pattern of investment has begun to decline. …Even if the point of diminishing returns to our present form of industrialism has not yet been reached, that point will inevitably arrive'. He ended with the dry observation: 'However much we like to think of ourselves as something special in world history, in fact industrial societies are subject to the same principles that caused earlier societies to collapse. If civilization collapses again, it will be from failure to take advantage of the current reprieve, a reprieve paradoxically both detrimental and essential to our anticipated future'.[26]

Persisting with architecture as if it is business as usual, could also be described as detrimental and essential to our anticipated future. Iconic projects are quite obviously subject to the law of diminishing returns. The costs, which have always been high, increasingly outweigh the effect they achieve. Nowhere is that clearer than in the race to the sky. After the 828 metres of the Burj Khalifa, the kilometre beckons, and the still unattained limit of Frank Lloyd Wright's 1956 Mile High Tower will also undoubtedly resurface. In terms of form, too, a limit seems to be in sight for all those curves, bulges and gravity-defying shapes.

Whether this iconic race will serve to advance architecture or the world, cannot automatically be answered in the affirmative. But for a generation of starchitects, currently sitting pretty at the top of the food chain, there is probably nothing for it but to persist in this march forward (and upward) in order to maintain their position as alpha males and (in a single instance) females.

At the other end of the spectrum are new generations of do-gooders who do not take part in this rat race, fully aware that there is little likelihood that they themselves will ever end up at the top of the food chain. They are searching for a different and modest biotope that can often no longer even be called architecture, but for which the term 'spatial agency' has been coined, based on the premise that even without building (a lot), it is still possible to bring about great change.[27]

Between these two extremes are the mass of architects who busy themselves with the bulk of construction in a role that no longer consists of overseeing the entire process from design to detailing to site supervision. In many cases bulk architects are little more than aesthetic consultants for complex real estate plans. What they do, is cut their coat according to their cloth, make the best of what they have, and continue designing buildings as best they can.

Given the current economic and demographic developments, Europe needs far fewer such buildings than in the past. Of course, there's nothing to stop architects

27.
Nishat Awan, Tatjana Schneider and Jeremy Till, *Spatial Agency: Other Ways of Doing Architecture*, London/New York 2011.

clinging to the idea that even if we have reached the end of large-scale new construction, there will always be spatial and programmatic issues that no one is better capable of solving than an architect. Whether that produces a building, or an intervention in which no materials are involved, doesn't really matter all that much. Furthermore, there are a great many buildings that need to be maintained, restored, renovated or converted. And of course the exceptional commissions continue to exist, just as they existed before the Industrial Revolution, when the mass of architects were not yet shaping society, but one or two of their number designed symbols of ecclesiastical and secular power.

That a more limited task requires fewer architects than the half million in Europe alone, is obvious. Just as obvious is the fact that not all the surplus architects are suddenly going to find new employment in the emerging economies. Brazil has eighty thousand of its own. Besides, the average architect in a BRICS country has more or less the same status as in deregulated Europe, so to the extent that there is any work for them, it is probably not much better that what is still to be found here.

For everyone who grew up with the mental reference of an inseparable link between growth and progress, it is barely conceivable that instead of more architecture there will be less. How difficult this is to imagine, is also evident in the educational institutions, which keep on turning out cohorts of architecture students on the assumption that as long as the world population grows and more and more people live in the city, the demand for architects will surely continue undiminished. However, there is a long list of professions that are dying out and of activities that have been made redundant by new technology, or that the West simply outsources to countries with lower wages and less strict environmental laws. The same thing could also happen with the

Wong Tung & Partners, MGM Grand casino, Macau, China, 2007.

architectural profession. Just as the industrial era destroyed or marginalized handwork and crafts, so the post-industrial era is seeing the disappearance of all manner of industries and occupations. Who could have foreseen thirty years ago that post offices would become superfluous?

A world where there is less new architecture is difficult to imagine from the perspective of the European architect, who lives with the idea of growth and progress, and who reflexively solves every problem by adding more cubic metres. A world in which no architecture is made is no doubt as unimaginable for an architect as a world in which no books are made is for a writer. And yet, if 95 per cent of the world can make do without architects, surely it is possible, even if only as a thought experiment, to imagine a world completely without architecture? Out of nothing, from zero and without preconceptions, it may be possible to envisage in that world a new practice that is no mere derivative, no feeble reflection, of architecture as we know it, a practice in which yesterday's all-encompassing generalists, freed from the frustration of being used for little more than the production of seductive images, can develop a new consciousness and reinvent themselves.

Moscow City, Moscow, Russia.

# FOURTH
# BRICS Summit
## March 29, 2012 : New Delhi

The 2012 BRICS summit, New Delhi, India.

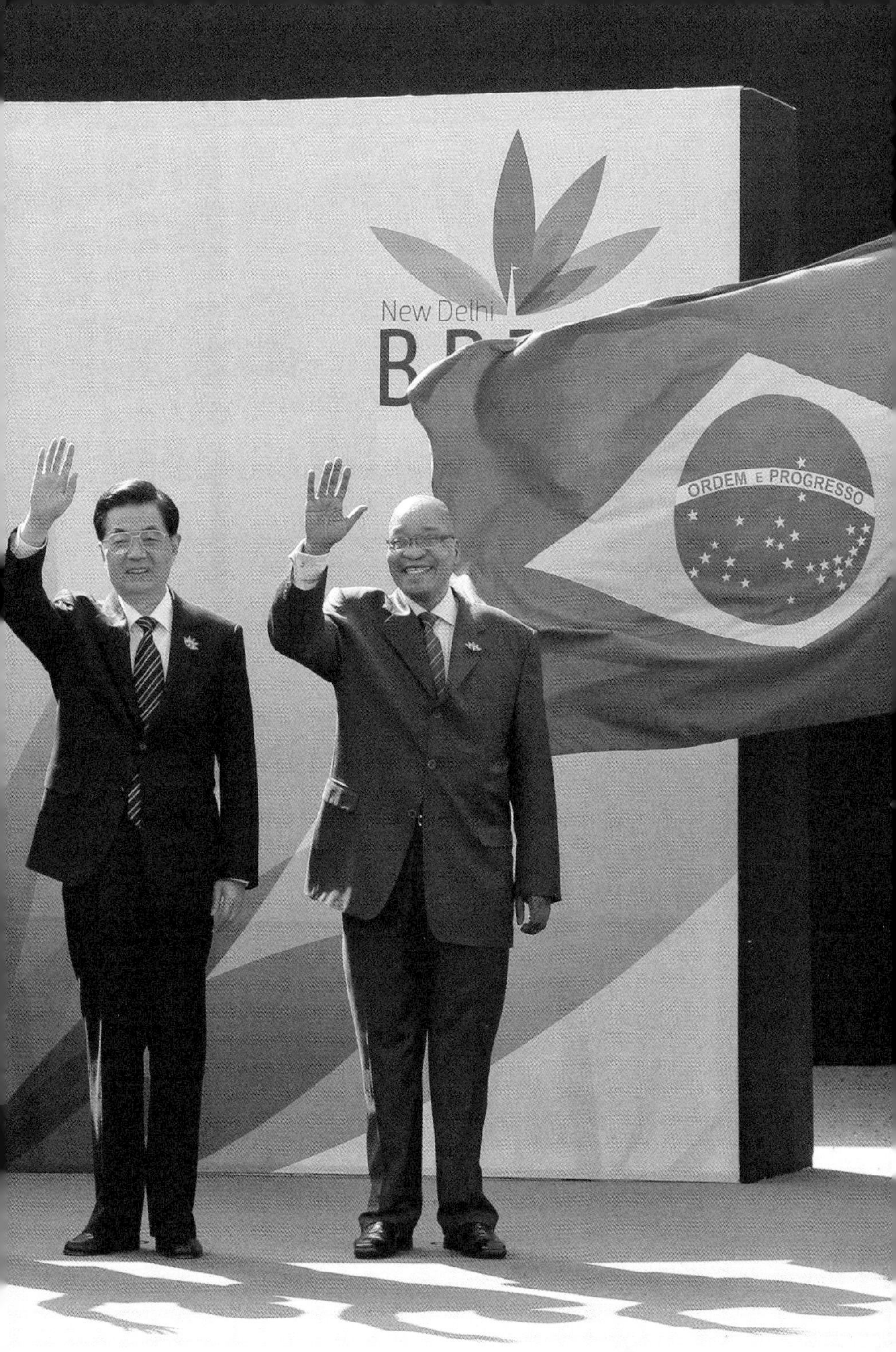

New Delhi
ORDEM E PROGRESSO

Renzo Piano Building Workshop,
The Shard, London, 2012.

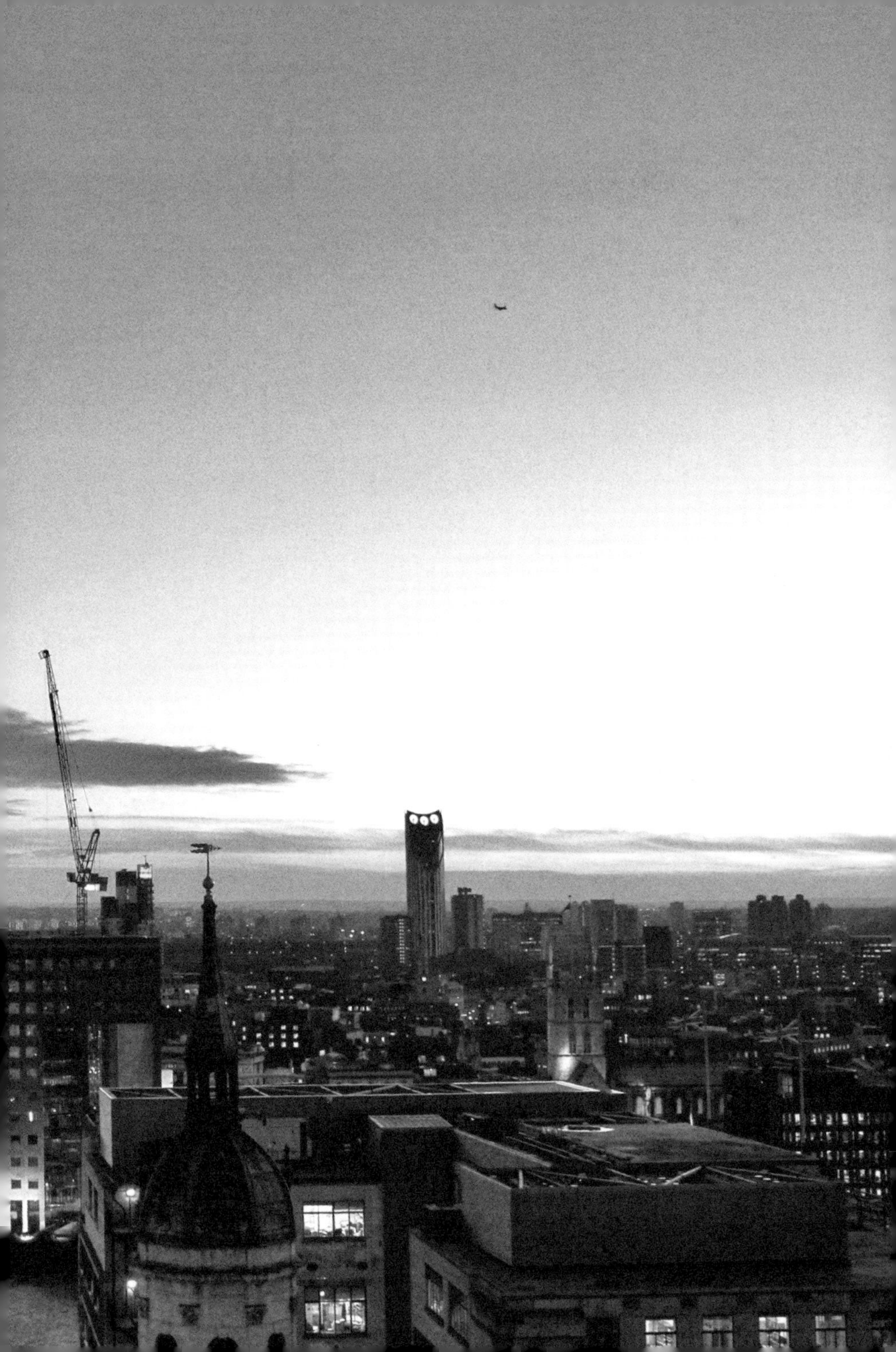

# CATALOGUE

# SINKING AND RISING

The balance of trade is the difference between the monetary value of exports and imports of output in an economy over a certain period. It is the relationship between a nation's imports and exports. A positive balance is known as a trade surplus if it consists of exporting more than is imported; a negative balance is referred to as a trade deficit or, informally, a trade gap. Both the United States and the European Union have had a string of trade deficits since the start of 21st century, while BRIC countries have created a growing trade surplus.

Source: IMF

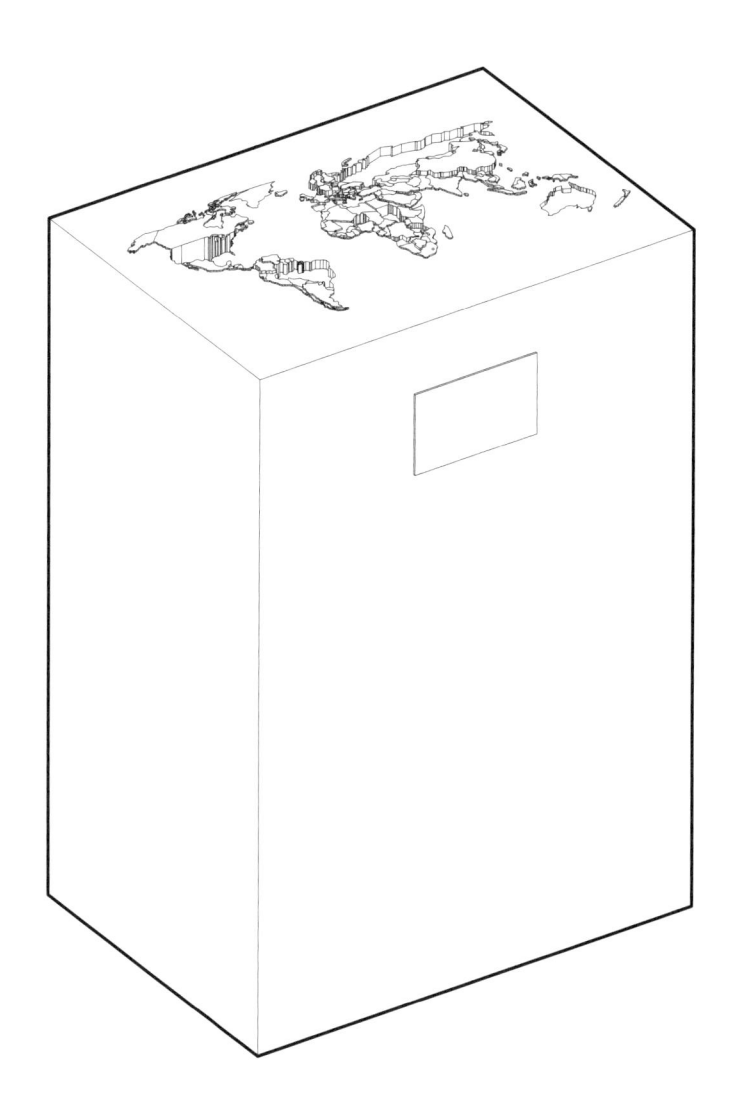

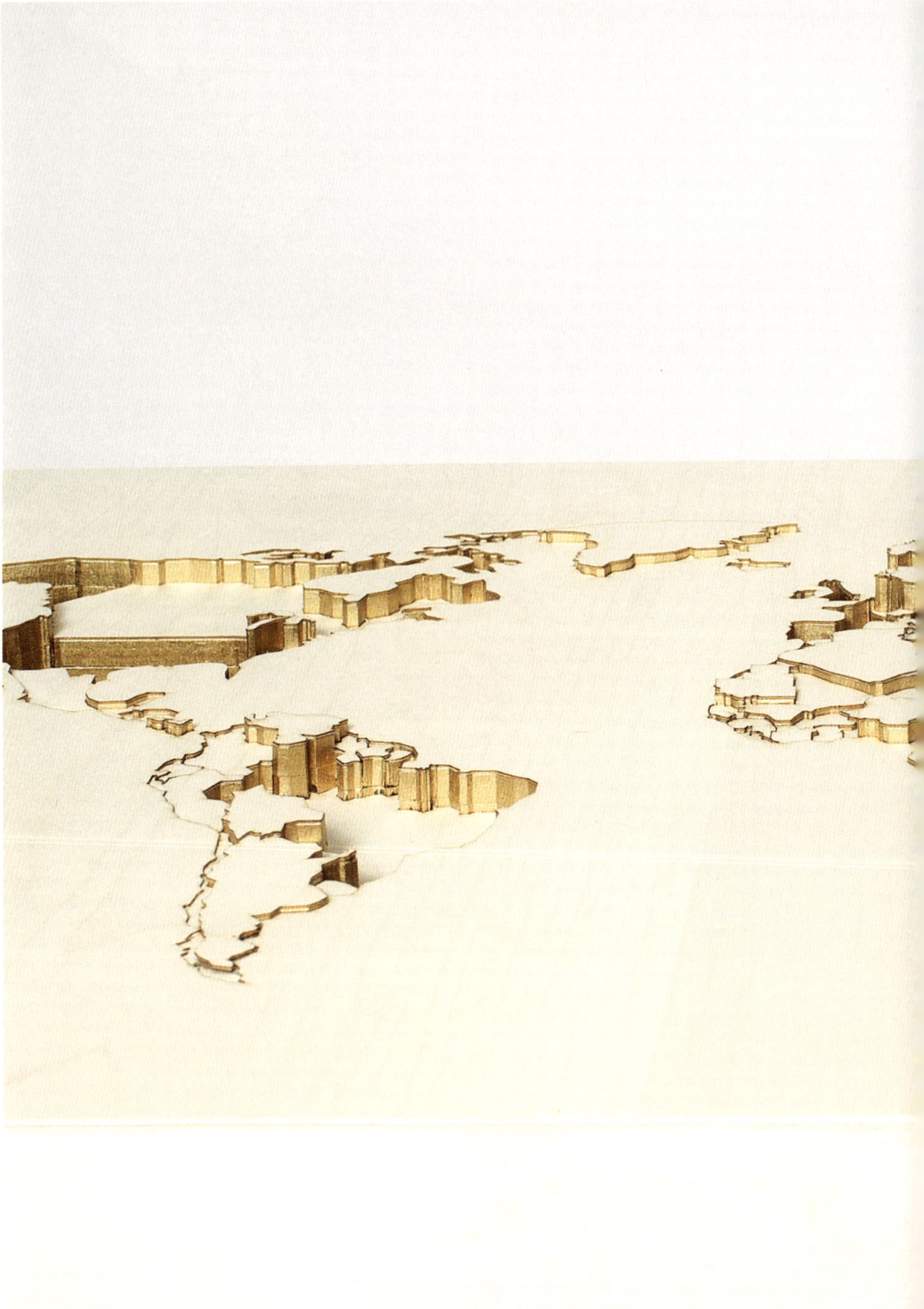

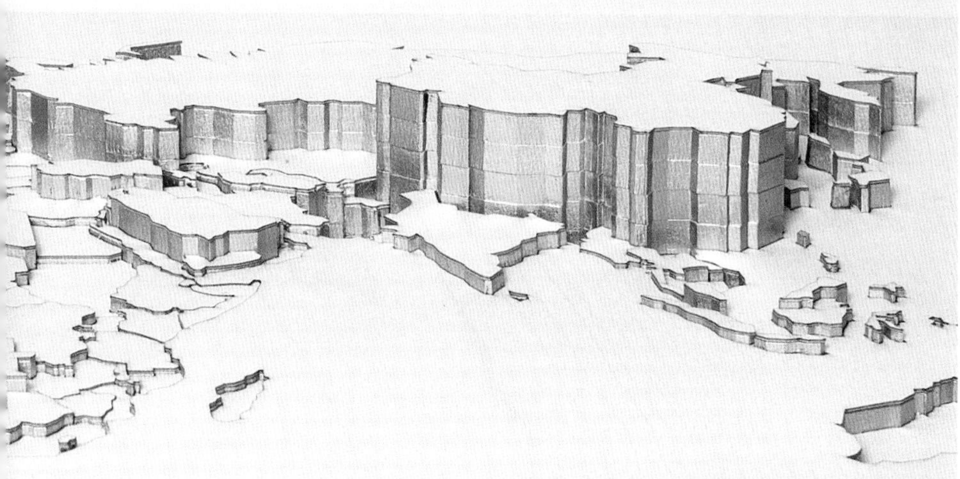

# BUBBLES

If there is one lesson to be learned from economic history it is that bubbles increase in size and frequency. This model shows the impact of financial bubbles, busts and crises on the world economy since 1900, per continent in relative scale to one another. The size of bubbles prior to 1900 is speculative since the available economic data makes it impossible to scale accurately.

Sources: www.stockcharts.com; www.imf.org

73

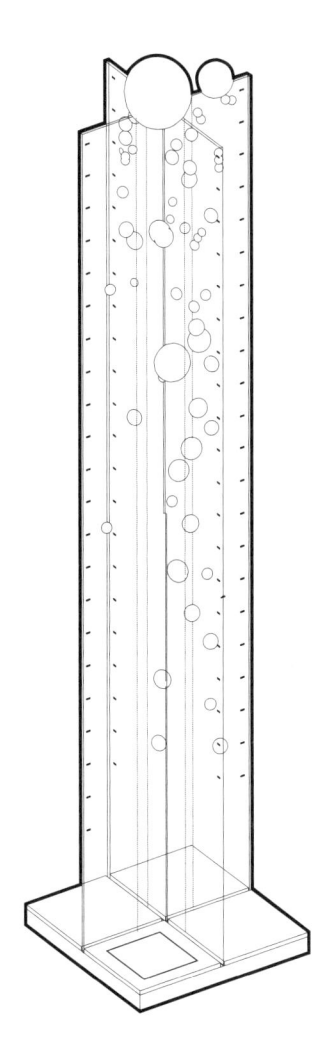

2010

Global Financial Crisis

2000

Brazilian Banking Crisis

Uruguay Banking Crisis

Russian Financial Crisis

Currency Crisis

1990

Iraq Invades Kuwait

Latin American Debt Crisis

2010

Europe debt crisis
Icelandic Financial Crisis

Dutch Banking Crisis

Irish Banking Crisis

Russian Financial Crisis

The Chinese Correction

The Dot Com Bubble 2000

2000

Hong Kong Financial Crisis

Y2K Millenium Bug

Asian Financial Crisis

2000

Black Wednesday Britian

Thailand Currency Devaluation

Black Monday
(Oct 19, 1987)

Finnish Banking Crisis

1990

Japanese Asset Price B

1990

Swedish Financial Crisis

## PROPERTY PRICES

Over recent decades house prices have soared in various countries, creating sudden spikes in real estate value, which rises faster than median personal income in those countries. At the peak of the bubble, houses in some countries 'earned' more money per year than the people living in them. This model shows the average growth in house prices measured against the average growth in (inflation corrected) income in eight different countries in the world.

Sources: CBS, www.economist.com

77

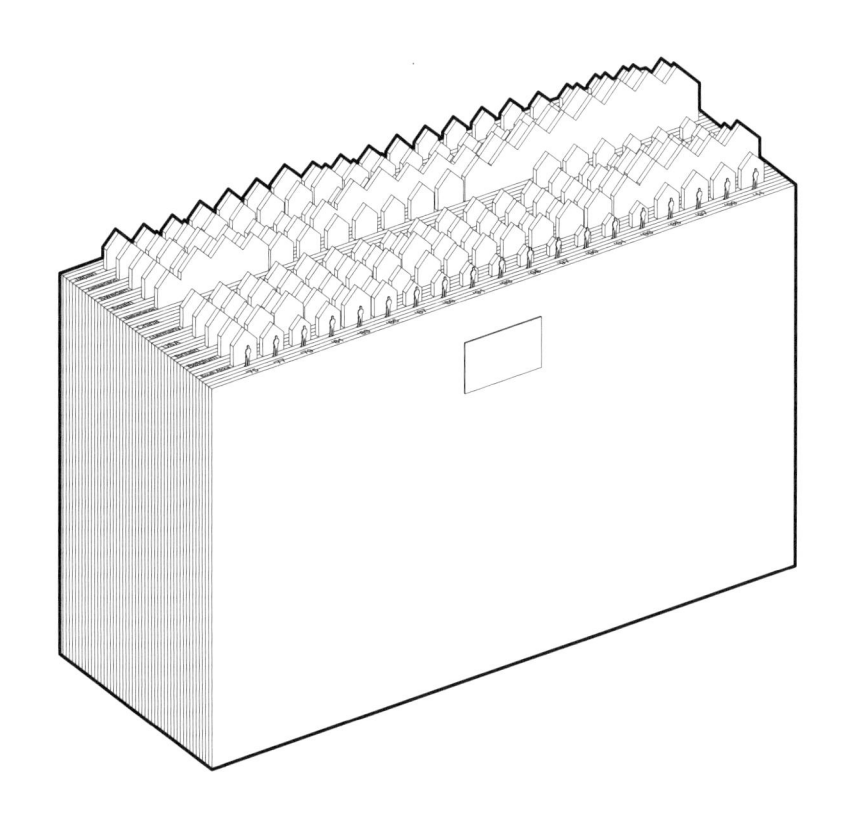

1983  1985  1987  1989  1991  199

1995 1997 1999 2001 2003 2005

# OUT OF BALANCE

In 2007 the standard leverage on a bank loan was a factor of 10, meaning that it was possible to borrow 10 times the value of the asset you were willing to offer in return. For investment banks themselves, however, different and far more risky leverages were created, rising to a factor of 67 for UBS. Even this figure is considered by economists to be a low estimate, as ingenious financial constructions may have pushed the actual factor still higher. After the introduction of the new banking regulations established by Basel III, the leverage of most banks returned to more reasonable levels in 2011.

Source: Centre of European Policy Studies; www.voxeu.org

81

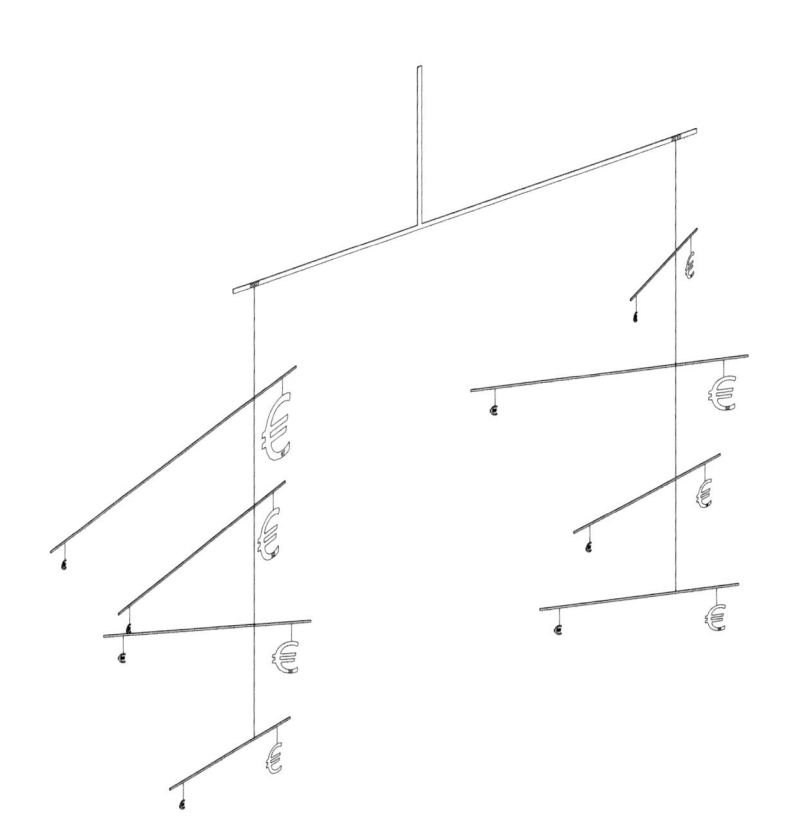

# RIDING THE WAVE

The European baby boomer generation, born between 1945 and 1955, was the last big European generation. This generation marks the end of a long period of strong population growth in Europe. At the same time, because of its size, the baby boomer generation spawned a Zeitgeist momentum of revolutionary cultural and social events as its members grew up – from the May '68 revolutions to the invention the Third Way politics of the nineties, and from the invention of the contraceptive pill to the invention of Viagra.

Sources: Eurostat, www.historycentral.com

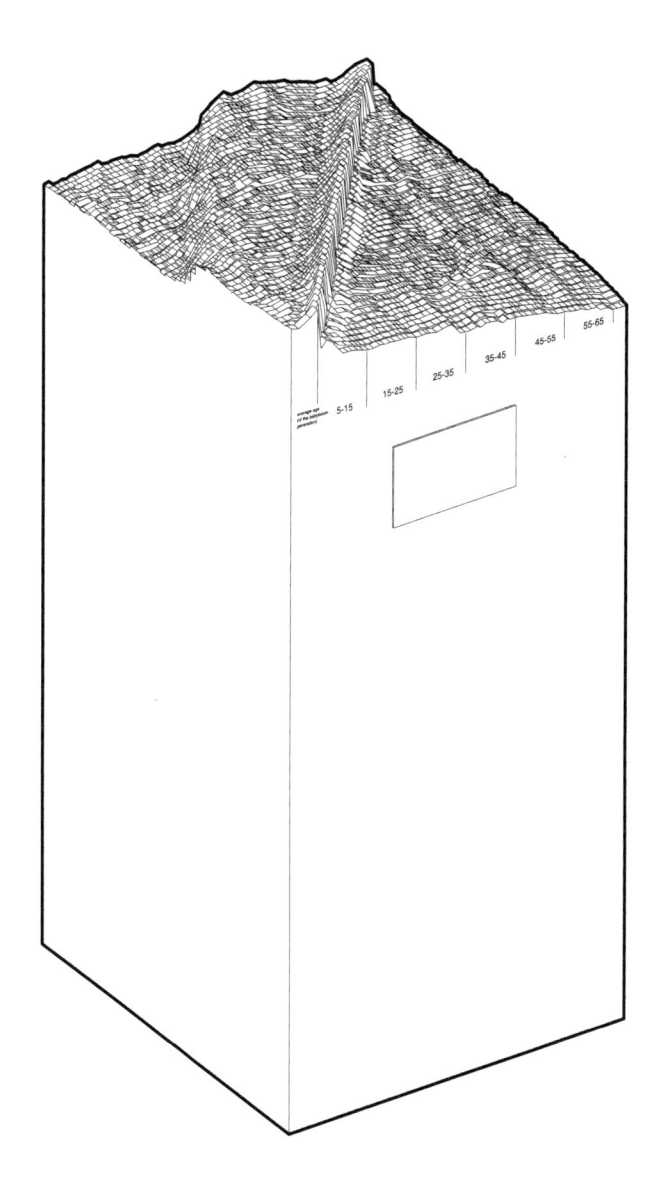

5-15  15-25  25-35  35-45  45-55  55-65

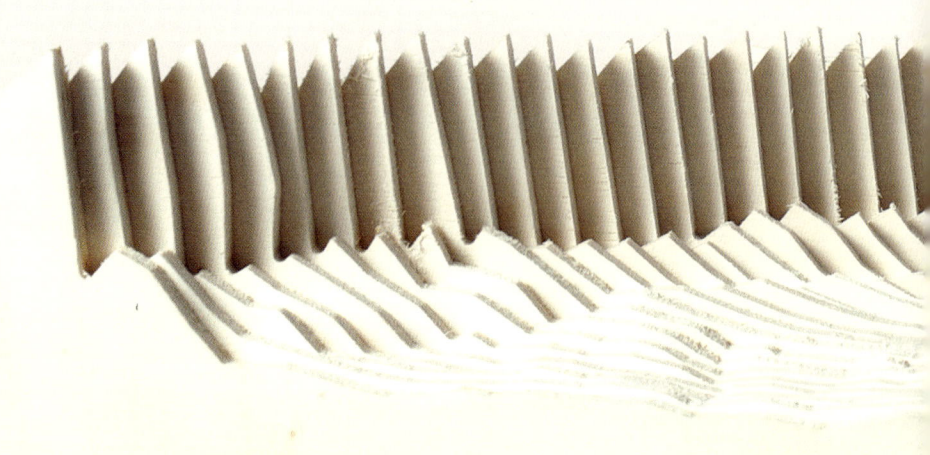

5-15         15-25         25-35

35-45    45-55    55-65

# DESIGNED BY ARCHITECTS

No more than 5% of buildings worldwide are designed by architects. Given an involvement in no more than five per cent of the built environment, architects do not have the power at a global level to exert genuine influence. Even in Europe, where the percentage of architecture with architects is higher, the role of the architect is limited. Deregulation has only served to limit it still further. As a result, the position of the European architect is fast becoming as marginal as that of architects in the rest of the world.

Source: Marcel Vellinga, Paul Oliver and Alexander Bridge, *Atlas of Vernacular Architecture of the World*, London 2008.

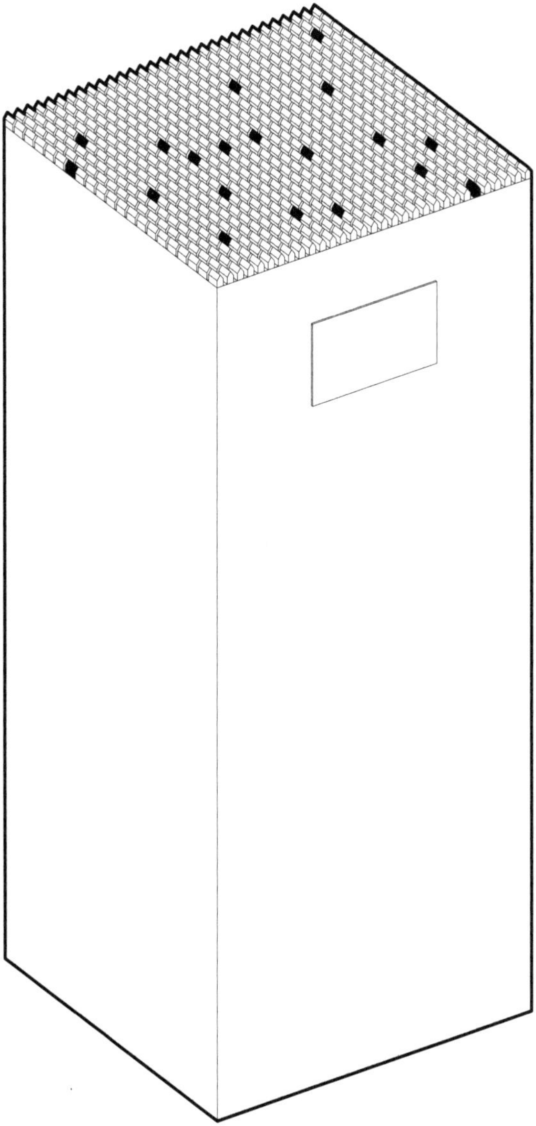

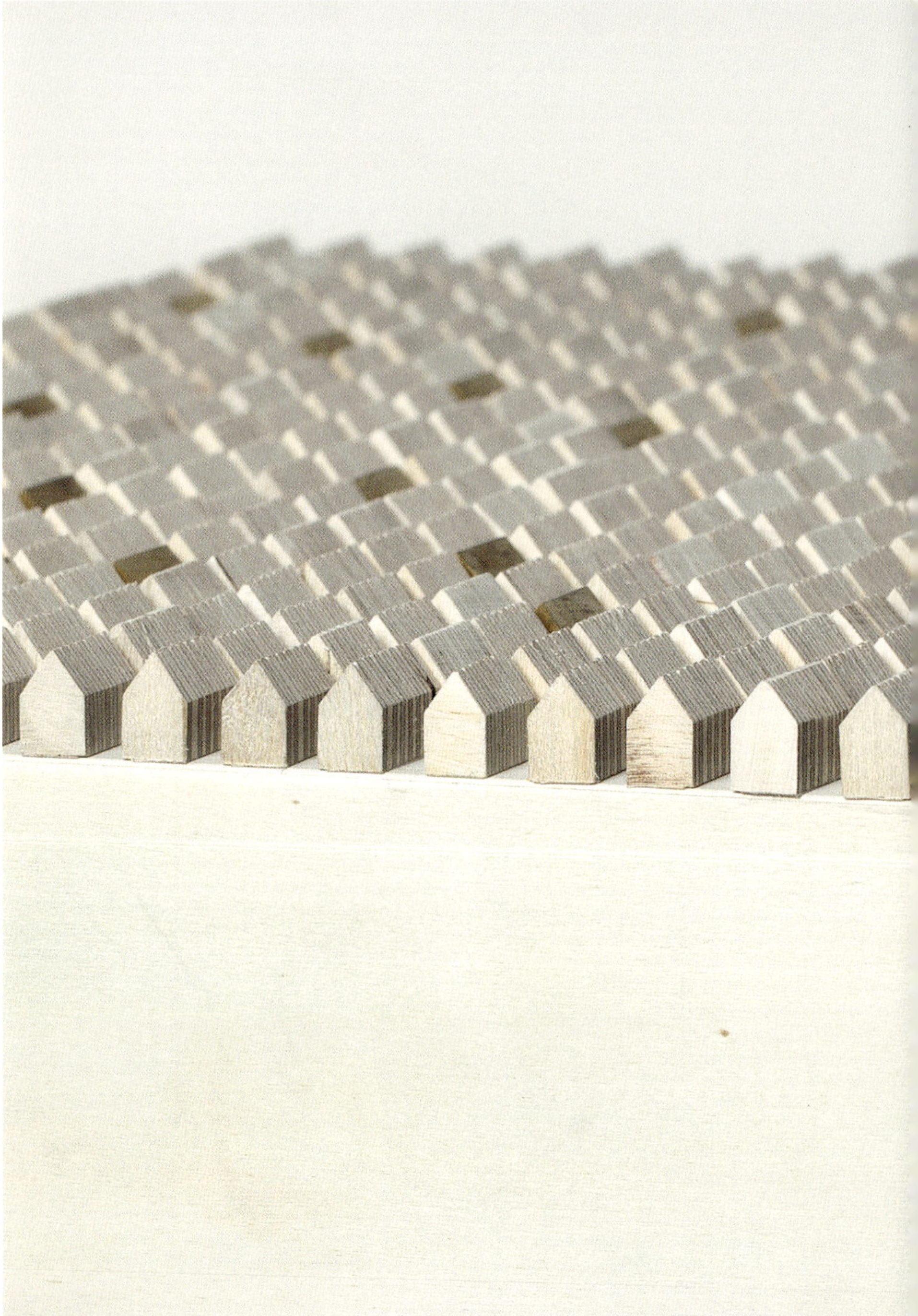

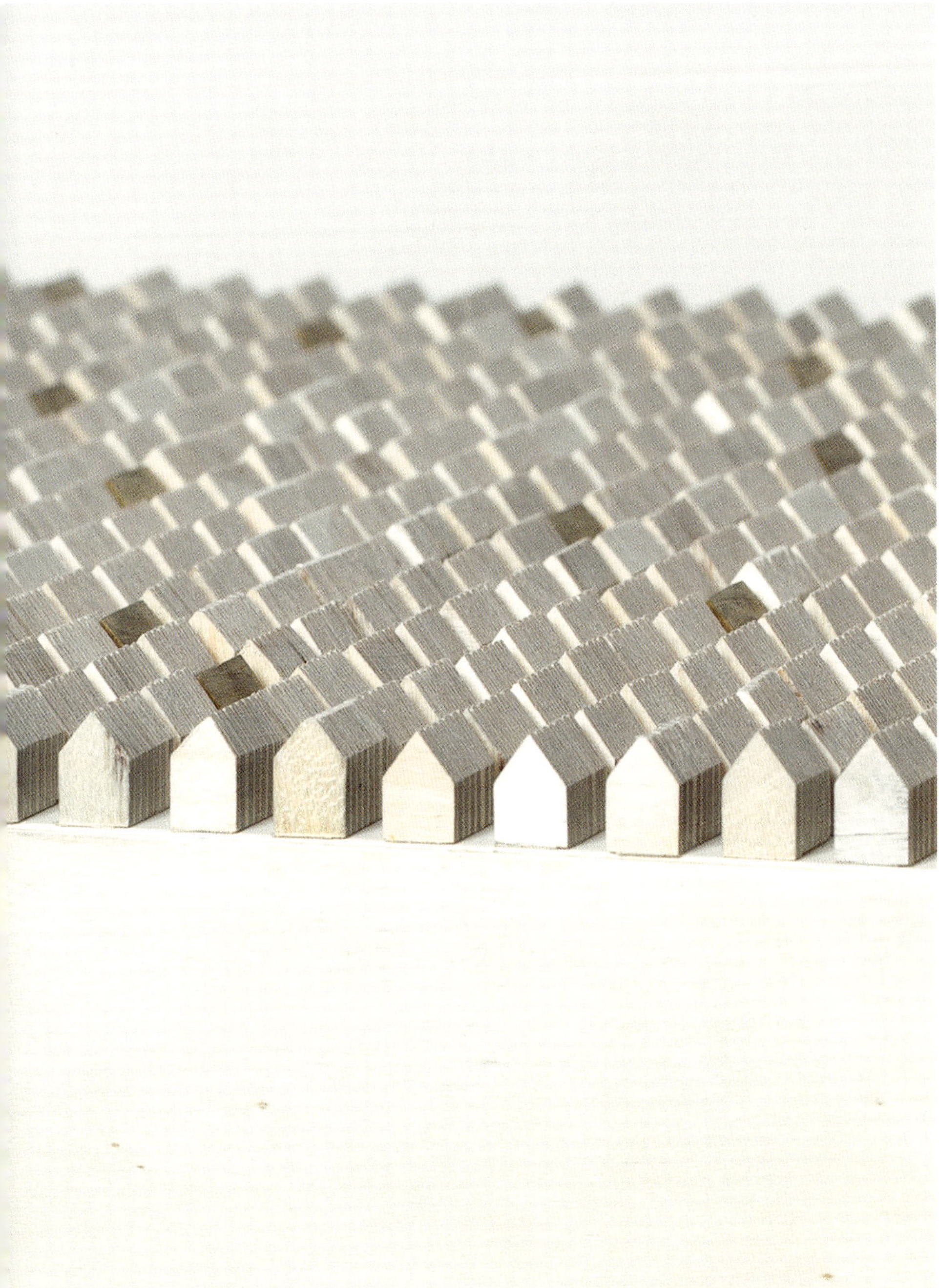

# DEMOGRAPHIC GROWTH

While Europe and North America have enjoyed strong population growth since the 19th century, this growth came to a halt at the end of the 20th century.
In China on the other hand the population started to grow during the last century and its growth peak is not yet in sight. While Europe had the biggest share of world population in the 19th century, it was first overtaken by the United States, which was itself soon overtaken by China. The next population champion will be sub-Saharan Africa, where countries like Nigeria are booming demographically.

Source: www.un.org

1700  1750  1800  1850  1900  1950  2000  2050

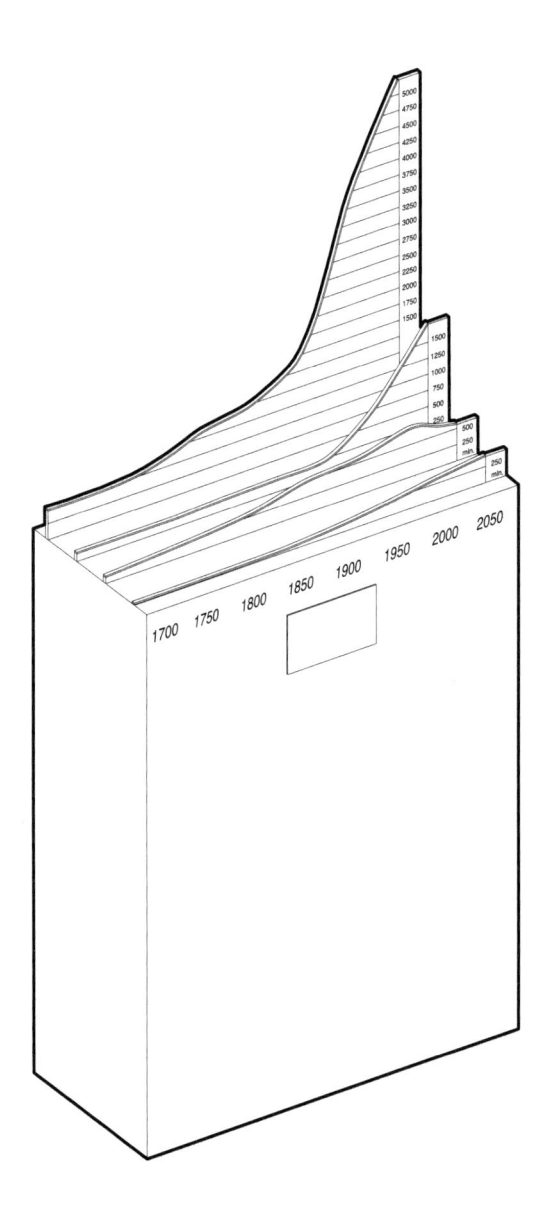

1700  1750  180

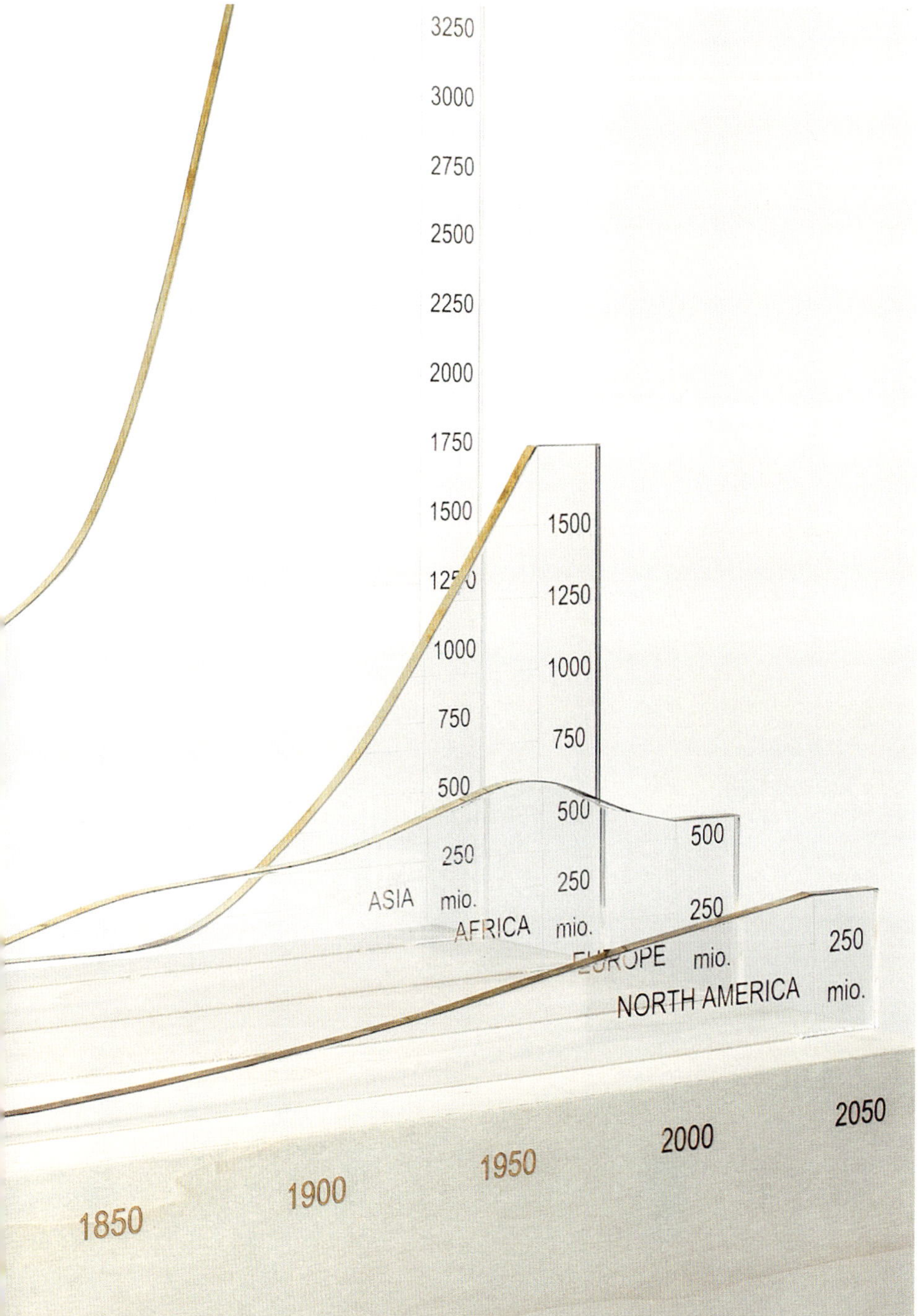
3250
3000
2750
2500
2250
2000
1750
1500
1250
1000
750
500
250
ASIA
mio.
1500
1250
1000
750
500
250
AFRICA
mio.
500
250
EUROPE
mio.
250
NORTH AMERICA
mio.
1850
1900
1950
2000
2050

# CREDITS

**Compilation**
Powerhouse Company
(Charles Bessard, Nanne
de Ru) and Hans Ibelings

**Models**
Sybren Woudstra,
Bjørn Andreassen and
Made by mistake

**Translation**
Robyn de Jong-Dalziel

**Graphic design**
Haller Brun, Amsterdam

**Printing**
Rotor, Ouderkerk a/d Amstel

**Published by**
The Architecture Observer,
Amsterdam/Montreal
www.architectureobserver.eu

This publication is supported by the Royal Netherlands Embassy, London

It was not possible to find all copyright holders of the illustrations used. Interested parties are requested to contact the publisher.

© 2012, The Architecture Observer and Powerhouse Company
All rights reserved. Reproduction in whole or part without prior written permission is prohibited.

ISBN 978-90-819207-0-4

**Image credits**
Christian van der Kooy: cover, pp. 70–71, 74–75, 78–79, 82–83, 86–87, 90–91, 94–95; Dominic Stevens/irish-vernacular.com: p. 41; Wikimedia Commons/Agência Brasil (José Cruz): pp. 22–23; Wikimedia Commons/Agência Brasil: pp. 62–63; Wikimedia Commons/Amjran: p. 26; Wikimedia Commons/Almc1217: p. 41 top right; Wikimedia Commons/AngMoKio: p. 41 bottom left; Wikimedia Commons/Júlio Boaro, pp. 20–21; Wikimedia Commons/Chilian Government: pp. 38–39; Wikimedia Commons/Christopherblack30: pp. 64–65; Wikimedia Commons/Eddylandzaat: p.18; Wikimedia Commons/JeCCo: pp. 36–37; Wikimedia Commons/Mimar77: p. 27; Wikimedia Commons/Krupasindhu Muduli: p. 41 bottom right; Wikimedia Commons/NARA: p 55; Wikimedia Commons/Nepenthes: p. 41 top left; Wikimedia Commons/NVO: p. 61; Wikimedia Commons/The Official White House Photostream (Peter Souza): pp.10–11; Wikimedia Commons/Presidencia de la Nación Argentina, pp. 50–51; Wikimedia Commons/Ricky Qi: pp. 48–49; Wikimedia Commons/Nicolas Scheuer: p. 8–9; Wikimedia Commons/simplifica: p. 19; Wikimedia Commons/Slowking4: p. 28; Wikimedia Commons/WiNG: p. 60.